To our parents, children, grandchildren, and extended family.

And to all those who have suffered from bipolar disorder.
We recognize your talent and great potential. May you
find meditation to be a valuable tool for opening your
heart and mind to positive change—and transcend.

"Annellen and Alex Simpkins have produced another great book that represents their lifelong commitment to helping people using unique resources. . . . This step-by-step guide of systematic meditation techniques is designed for people diagnosed with bipolar disorder. The reader learns to enter into a different mental state that permits both relaxation and alertness, where once there was only mania or despair."

—**Michele Ritterman, PhD**, *world lecturer on "The Three-Minute Trance," and author of The Tao of a Woman and Using Hypnosis in Family Therapy*

"The Simpkins have written a wonderful book. It begins with a solid foundation of ancient Eastern philosophy integrated with modern Western science and a clear description of bipolar disorder. The benefits of a variety of meditations are described and clear guidelines are offered to match these with the individual symptoms that different people experience. Simple, easy-to-follow exercises are offered throughout the book so each reader can experience their own process, leading to sustained improvements. This is a wonderful book and will be appreciated by many people suffering from bipolar disorder. I recommend it enthusiastically."

—**Robert McNeilly, MBBS**, *an international teacher of Ericksonian approaches to psychotherapy and hypnosis*

"A wonderfully well-written book integrating ancient philosophy of Tao and modern neuroscience for self-help with bipolar disorder."

—**Kathryn and Ernest Rossi**, *authors of the video e-book Creating New Consciousness in Everyday Life*

"*The Tao of Bipolar* is a how-to guide to clearing your mind, easing your moods, and developing your talents. I'm pleased to have this powerful resource to offer to my patients. The Simpkins offer you the tools you need to gain a high level of awareness and control over your bipolar symptoms. Their easy explanations and practical meditation exercises will help you develop powerful, life-changing habits."

—**Ashley Davis Bush, LCSW**, *author of Shortcuts to Inner Peace and Transcending Loss*

"Even though the book is mainly directed to persons with bipolar disorders, it is also helpful for any therapist. The book nurtures the mind, body, and spirit of every reader; satisfies the need for sound knowledge; and gives the pleasure of reading a well-written book enriched by metaphors and cases that enhance the passionate hope that the meditations proposed in the book really work. . . . The deep message the book conveys is: Nurture your potential by committing yourself to doing the meditations. Find healthy daily routines of waking and sleeping, balance your moods to harmonize your relationships, and become what you want to become, trusting in the power of both Tao and nature."

—**Consuelo Casula,** *psychologist, psychotherapist, and the president-elect of the European Society of Hypnosis*

"Throughout this helpful, holistic, clear, and cogent book the experienced authors skillfully depict both the bipolar condition and the many therapeutic ways its symptoms may be alleviated. Compassionately reassuring the sufferer, they encourage an attitude of non-judgmental awareness accomplished by meditation and breathing exercises to follow each day. . . . This book will be of great help to any who reads it and applies it to their lives."

—**Tasha Halpert**, *meditation teacher, columnist, blogger, and author of Heartwings: Love Notes for a Joyous Life*

"A true self-help book. The authors expertly guide the reader through a description of bipolar disorder and teach, step-by-step, how to meditate to increase the ability to manage the mood swings that go with bipolar disorder. A great introduction for anyone considering treatment, and a thoughtful addition to talk and medication therapies."

—**Tanya H. Hess, PhD**, *director of training at Coaching into Care, Philadelphia VA Medical Center*

Contents

Introduction

Your bipolar disorder need not hold you back from accomplishing your goals and doing what you care about. Throughout the ages and into the present, many have suffered from bipolar disorder. And yet, a percentage of those who receive this diagnosis manage to accomplish great things and lead productive, happy lives. So can you!

Typically, people have a pessimistic view of bipolar disorder. You may have been told that bipolar disorder is a lifelong medical problem with a strong effect on the brain. As a result, you might be thinking there's not much you can do. But we invite you to join those who are successfully managing their bipolar disorder, by opening yourself to the idea that you *can* help yourself. If you catch a cold, you might believe that all you can do is endure it. But going out in the rain, missing sleep, or exposing yourself to other illnesses will certainly make things worse, whereas getting plenty of rest and drinking liquids will probably help. Most medical conditions, including bipolar disorder, can be improved when the patient takes an active role.

If you view a house only from the outside, you will never know what's inside. But after you enter the building, you can walk to all the different rooms within. Similarly, you may be thinking about bipolarity from an external perspective, based on the negative things people have told you. These pessimistic perspectives might keep you from trying to do anything to alter your condition. Meditation lights the lamp of your inner experience, thereby allowing you to guide your actions from an illuminated source within, whereby you will discover new potential and options for improving your life.

This book offers you an optimistic view of bipolar disorder drawn from the ancient wisdom of the East and combined with the latest findings on bipolar disorder from neuroscience, psychology, and Western medicine. You will look at your mood problems through a different lens. *Taoism* is an ancient philosophical tradition that focuses on the principle of harmony and balance known as the *Tao*, which can be found through meditation. By viewing your mood problems through the lens of the Tao, you add another perspective and many practical methods for improving your bipolar disorder. This time-honored perspective, with its meditation techniques, will bring you feelings of well-being, balance, and happiness. Your life will be enhanced as you live with greater awareness, and this book shows you how to do it.

What Are Moods?

Without your feelings and experiences, who are you? Emotions are like music, lending harmony or discord to experience. You can find examples all around you: When a good friend you rarely get to see visits, you spontaneously feel happy, even elated! Then, having shared some wonderful time together, you feel sad when that person has to leave. Eating your favorite food, you feel enjoyment, whereas when you take a sip of sour milk, you feel disgust. Each of these emotions occurs naturally in relation to what you are doing and experiencing, and all of them elicit your sense of meaning about the events in your life. Whether your feelings are positive or negative, they add information that deepens your understanding of yourself and the world. The emotional center of the brain, known as the *limbic system*, is highly interconnected with many different regions all around the nervous system. These extensive links help to explain why your feelings are so much a part of what you think and do.

When an emotion endures, it becomes a *mood*. Moods are also a way of knowing what's happening. For example, when people find themselves continually feeling irritable, it often reflects a problem in their lives. Then when the problem is solved, the irritable mood goes away. Emotions and moods are normal, built-in reactions of the mind-brain-body system. They come into being and then leave again as an integral part of everyday life. Through this process of experiencing continually changing emotions, we weave the cloth of our lives.

The
Tao of
Bipolar

Using Meditation & Mindfulness
to Find Balance & Peace

C. Alexander Simpkins, PhD
Annellen M. Simpkins, PhD

New Harbinger Publications, Inc.

Distributed in Canada by Raincoast Books

Copyright © 2013 by C. Alexander Simpkins and Annellen M. Simpkins
New Harbinger Publications, Inc.
5674 Shattuck Avenue
Oakland, CA 94609
www.newharbinger.com

Cover design by Amy Shoup
Acquired by Melissa Kirk
Edited by Nelda Street

Library of Congress Cataloging-in-Publication Data

Simpkins, C. Alexander.
  The tao of bipolar : using meditation and mindfulness to find balance and peace / C. Alexander Simpkins, PhD, and Annellen M. Simpkins, PhD.
      pages cm
  Includes bibliographical references.
  ISBN 978-1-60882-292-8 (pbk. : alk. paper) -- ISBN 978-1-60882-293-5 (pdf e-book) -- ISBN 978-1-60882-294-2 (epub) 1. Manic-depressive illness. 2. Manic-depressive illness--Treatment. 3. Tai chi. 4. Exercise therapy. I. Simpkins, Annellen M. II. Title.
  RC516.S563 2013
  616.89'5--dc23

                              2012047227

Printed in the United States of America

18   17   16

10   9   8   7   6   5   4   3

But when you have bipolar disorder, your emotions and moods don't always accurately reflect what's happening in your life. In fact, your moods may mislead you, creating problems for you. Your moods can be extreme, leading you into tangled knots in the fabric of your life experience and, at other times, tearing the fabric apart. If you suffer from the chronic moodiness found in bipolar disorder, your mood can take you on a roller-coaster ride from low to high and back again. You may become engulfed in a vortex of emotions that push and pull you away from any sense of calm and stability. As you work through this book, you will learn how to get off the roller coaster and return to more balanced emotions that can become a resource for you rather than a problem.

Bipolar Disorder, the Brain, and Meditation

Modern neuroscience has found that the brain continues to develop and change throughout adulthood, and that we can influence this development with our actions. Bipolar disorder has a strong brain component associated with mood swings. Research reveals that people with bipolar disorder have structural abnormalities in neural pathways that are involved in regulating moods (Strakowski et al. 1999). The mental training that comes from practicing meditation increases activation in the parts of the brain that manage emotions and moods. Regular meditation can make these important structures and connections even denser (Tang et al. 2009). These exciting findings and others that we will discuss in this book offer compelling evidence that meditation can change your brain and stabilize your moods.

Meditation also has many general benefits. You know that the symptoms of bipolar disorder can be extremely stressful for you and your family. Many different studies have found that meditators feel less stressed and anxious (Kabat-Zinn 2003), so you will be able to address your problems with more calm and comfort. Meditating also balances your autonomic nervous system (Grossman et al. 2004), which can lessen your tendency to swing from high to low and back again. And meditation is well known for inducing an overall experience of well-being (Lutz et al. 2009).

We encourage you to use meditation along with your drug therapy. The two treatments enhance each other. With all of these positive effects on your brain, mind, and body, you can find happiness and discover your own unique stability.

What This Book Offers

This book offers hope. It helps you to restore your faith in yourself. It gives you a clear path to follow. And it helps you develop your talents and express them realistically and effectively in the world. Using meditation allows your experience to become your teacher. You will be able to notice what's really going on. Through this awareness, you can learn more about what you need to do to live the life you want to live. You will develop tools for either activating or calming your mind, brain, and body to restore balance. When you are attuned to the moment, alert, aware, and at ease with yourself, you can express your best potential for living fully.

The book is divided into three parts. Part 1 presents a new perspective for understanding bipolarity, based on the Tao's ever-changing movement of flowing energy. From this perspective, you can use a set of meditative tools to alter this flow in order to bring about real mind-brain changes. You will learn the latest scientific knowledge about bipolar disorder and how meditation changes your brain. Part 2 teaches three forms of meditation step-by-step. *Focus meditations* train you to keep your attention deliberately focused on something, such as breathing, which helps you gain some control over your thought processes. *Open-focus meditations*, such as mindfulness, have an ever-changing object of focus that teaches you how to keep your attention flexible and aware. And *no-focus meditations* free your mind so that you can have clear, aware consciousness. Part 3 guides you in applying these skills to reduce your stress, manage your moods, improve your interpersonal relationships, and develop your talents and abilities. We often tell our clients that their problems are the seeds of their potential, and this part of the book helps you transform troubling symptoms into creative capabilities. We draw on well-researched methods and include stories of clients who used these techniques successfully.

What Is Meditation?

Meditation began long ago and has its roots in the ancient traditions from the East: yoga, Buddhism, Taoism, and Zen. Thousands of intelligent people from all around the world have contributed to the evolution of meditation through time. Today we have the fruits of more than two thousand years of sincere exploration, study, writings, and analysis in a rich and varied set of meditation practices.

Meditation is a time for sitting quietly, seemingly doing nothing. In the empty moment, you can discover meditation. You might think that sitting quietly and doing nothing is a waste of time. How can anything significant be accomplished by doing nothing? The answer requires a shift in how you look at things. Then, what at first seemed to be a non-activity is its own kind of action.

To understand what meditation is in general, you can get to know it better in terms of opposites. Meditation empties the mind of thoughts or fills it with chosen thoughts. Some meditations direct attention deliberately to an inner or outer object of focus, while others are indirect, objectless, and open ended. Meditation can withdraw attention from the outer world and focus it inwardly, or it can direct attention outward for alertness and awareness in every moment. This book guides you through the process.

Whom This Book Is For

This book is for anyone who is dealing with bipolar disorder or mood problems. You can use it as a self-help adjunct if you are in treatment and on medication. If you have not sought medical care but simply feel bothered by moodiness, you will also find this book helpful. Many of the meditations in this book will also assist you with the stress and disturbance that you may be feeling. You may want to share things you learn in this book with your parents, siblings, or spouse. Their support and positive attitude can help you to help yourself. With everyone working together, new potential opens up for all involved.

The meditation methods presented in this book offer powerful tools for change. As you gain mental skills and become mindful of what you are experiencing, you will be better able to take an active part in your own treatment. So these methods can work well with medical and psychological care.

We encourage you to seek a doctor or therapist and to use these methods in conjunction with medication when needed, along with a good diet, regular exercise, and adequate sleep. If you are having trouble maintaining these healthy habits, this book may help you to discover how to be healthy and in balance. And although meditation is something everyone usually can do, we recommend consulting a psychotherapist or physician who is familiar with this kind of approach before you begin, to ensure that you have no psychological or physical conditions that might preclude meditating. If you do have a history of severe anxiety, depression, or trauma, always use these methods under the guidance of a well-trained professional. When you work in conjunction with an expert, a better and happier life will open up for you!

How to Use This Book

This book offers things to read and think about, as well as exercises to practice. We encourage you to actually do the exercises. Although there are concepts, theories, and research findings, change takes place through your experience. By doing the exercises, you give yourself the opportunity to feel something new. Through the process of actively engaging in the exercises, change happens. You can skip around, especially in part 3, working with the sections that seem most relevant to your situation and needs.

When you do an exercise, read it through a few times. Then, set the book down and try the exercise. Begin with a short amount of time and gradually increase it. Even devoting a minute or two to meditation will help you feel better and start a change process. And as you become more skilled at meditating, you will be able to increase the amount of time you devote to it. Start where you are, with what's comfortable for you to do. Accept whatever you do without judging it as good or bad. Learning to accept things as they are is a primary quality of meditation. You will discover ways to stop being so hard on yourself as you engage in the meditative experience.

We have been writing about meditation for decades and have written numerous books on these rich and beautiful practices. We also teach meditation to the public and to other professionals to help them integrate this useful tool into their work. Over the years, we have come to respect the unique talents and creativity in our clients who have suffered from bipolar disorder. We have developed meditative treatments to help them stop dissipating their energy so that they can focus it on developing their potential. It is our sincere hope that you will cultivate your best qualities as you work with this book.

Part 1

Fundamental Principles and Facts

Chapter 1

Looking through the Lens of the Tao

This chapter introduces fundamental principles from Eastern healing that can help you begin the process of overcoming the problems from your bipolar disorder. The exercises that accompany each principle help you to experience the ideas personally. You will gain a better understanding of the nature of bipolar according to the Tao, which opens up a new way of working with your bipolar disorder.

What Is the Tao?

Tao means "way," a path or method to follow. And that path is the way things are, their essential nature. Each thing has its own Tao, its way. When you attune to the way things are, you gain understanding and access. Then, everything you do flows more easily. Often when people have a problem, they think the best way to overcome it is to set it at a distance and fight against it. And of course, it makes sense to try to overcome your problems with bipolar disorder. But how to do so successfully may not be what you expect.

Taoism teaches that the way to overcome problems is to first get to know them. Begin by moving closer, aligning with the underlying forces instead of fighting against them. Use your awareness to help you redirect the flow of energy and bring about change. Thus, the first step is to get to know what you are working with, your personal Tao, or way, and the

Tao of your bipolar disorder. You do this by tuning in meditatively, and this book will show you how. This ancient wisdom can help you to cope better with your bipolar disorder.

According to the ancient Taoist classic, the Tao Te Ching, before the beginning of the world as we know it today, there was the Tao, an undifferentiated, endless emptiness with no beginning and no end. But with the beginning of the world, this emptiness began to take form. The emergence of the Tao in the world is often pictured as an empty circle with a dotted outline, shown barely emerging from the background. The Tao in its undifferentiated form is the foundation that sets everything in motion. From its unformed beginnings, the Tao evolved into the complex patterns that form our world.

The Tao, as an empty void, is the wellspring, so emptiness is not simply "nothing." In emptiness, we find openness filled with potential. Life springs from the Tao. We see the importance of emptiness everywhere around us. For example, a cup would not be what it is without the empty space inside it. Once you fill a cup—perhaps you decide to fill it with soil, to make a planter—it loses its capacity as a cup. Emptiness is essential for a cup to serve its function as a vessel to be filled.

When you learn how to meditate, you return to emptiness, the undifferentiated Tao, where you can find your path to follow. The Tao Te Ching states, "Take emptiness to the limit; maintain tranquility in the center" (Lao-tzu 1989, 68). In those moments of silence, you open a space for the Tao to appear. Emptiness may seem like a vague foundation, but as you discover your own open moments through meditation, you will learn that the pushes and pulls that have ruled your life fade away, leaving an empty space for new possibilities to take form.

Exercise 1.1   Discover an Empty Moment

Set a timer on your watch or clock for one minute. Find a comfortable place to sit down. Just sit quietly. Do nothing except sit quietly. Let your breathing be relaxed and comfortable. If you find yourself feeling as if you should be doing something, gently remind yourself that you are just sitting quietly, and return to sitting and doing nothing. In this silent, empty moment, with nothing that needs to be done, you open a space for something new to happen.

Attuning to Your Personal Tao

You have your own Tao, your personal way. Your personality; your likes and dislikes; your thoughts, behaviors, and feelings emerge spontaneously as an expression of your deeper nature, your Tao. You spontaneously expressed your Tao as a child, when you found yourself drawn to some activities and not others. For example, our love of writing began early, when we were children: Annellen created "Things to Do" books for family and friends, and Alex designed, wrote, and produced his own newspaper. As we mention our early interests, you will probably think of yours. Perhaps you liked to play sports or video games, or maybe you were happiest with a box of crayons and a pad of paper. Children express their Tao naturally, and sometimes these early interests give you clues about your deeper nature.

Exercise 1.2   Uncover Your Personal Tao

Think about your interests throughout your life. What did you like to do when you were a child? What was your favorite subject in school? What did you do best? Were you athletic, artistic, or perhaps social? Now consider what you like to do as an adult. What do you choose to do when there's nothing that you have to do? What are your hobbies? Whether or not you pursue these interests seriously, consider what they are. As you think about these things, you can begin to recognize that you are much more than your bipolar disorder. True, it pushes and pulls you strongly, but you also have many interests, tendencies, and talents that comprise your fuller nature, your Tao. Your Tao is a constant center that guides the journey of your life. And by taking the time to become aware of yourself in this way, you will gain tangible skills that will prove helpful in overcoming your problems from bipolar disorder.

Attuning to the Tao of Bipolar

As you might expect, bipolar disorder has its own Tao, its way. In the West we typically define disorders by their symptoms, and bipolar disorder is typically depicted as swings in moods, work disturbances, and loss of sleep. These are the outer manifestations of the disorder. But the Eastern way looks for the source, the deeper nature that drives the symptoms. So, you might be wondering, what is the essence of bipolar disorder, its Tao?

The Tao of bipolar disorder affects energy. At its core, bipolar disorder involves a cyclical change of energy. The original name, *manic depression*, was replaced with the term *bipolar disorder*. Experts recognized that the problem was better understood as an energy or mood change along a continuum (see chapter 2). Therefore, learning about the nature of change itself (described in the next section) will give you deeper insight into your mood shifts. To truly know the Tao of bipolar disorder means to become aware of your energy as it undergoes change. Then you will be able to move your energy toward a natural balance that flows smoothly through time.

You can work with your bipolar disorder by attuning to yourself in real time as you undergo changes in energy. Through the practice of meditation, you gain skills that will help you become aware of your shifts in energy. You will learn how to notice changes in your energy as they happen, moment by moment. You will be able to sustain your awareness to notice the flow of energy, because it is ongoing. And by becoming mindfully aware of these subtle, underlying forces that drive your mood swings, you will be able to recognize the source and work from it in order to lessen your troubling symptoms.

Following the Way of Nonaction

Then how do you implement this real-time attuning to the Tao of your bipolar disorder? One of the key teachings in the Tao Te Ching is the way of nonaction: *wu wei*. Take no action, and then nothing will remain undone. You might wonder, *How can I make a significant change in my problems without doing something to make it happen?* Penetrating deeper into the meaning of nonaction offers creative alternatives to typical ways of trying to make things happen.

The Tao Te Ching states that the first step on the way to the Tao is to be in harmony with, not in rebellion against, the fundamental laws of the universe (Waley 1958). Thus, the first step in overcoming the symptoms of bipolar disorder is to become aware of yourself along with your levels of energy and corresponding thoughts, feelings, and behaviors. Although your intention is to change, you begin by noticing yourself just as you are. With this awareness, you will gain a certain amount of control. So, even though your symptoms, at times, may feel all encompassing and completely out of your control, your awareness inserts a new variable, and with it comes the potential for change.

Now you can probably see that nonaction doesn't mean that you literally should do nothing at all to try to help yourself. Instead, it means that you don't take any action that is contrary to the deeper nature of the situation. You might typically think of taking action to improve your mood as forcing yourself to feel a different way. Or maybe your mood is just a reaction to how you are feeling, and you can't quite help it. The Taoist way involves neither trying to take action nor just reacting. The action you take should be in accord with the forces at play. You don't have to try to oppose your mood, nor do you have to just resign yourself to feeling discomfort. Instead, you learn to follow your mood and use its force to redirect it in a better direction. This means starting with awareness. Notice the forces and sense their direction. Then, like an experienced logger who can guide logs downstream with the current, you will be able to channel your energy to help you accomplish your goals.

Learning to take a path of nonaction with problems is more effective than avoiding them or fighting against them. Phobias are a good example of the power of nonaction. People often try to manage the fear by running away from it. But the more they do things to avoid their fear, the worse it gets. And as a result, they lose touch with the real situation. From the perspective of nonaction, they have lost their attunement to the feared situation's true nature. An effective form of treatment for phobias, known as *exposure therapy*, involves staying with the fear. Being calmly immersed in the situation without trying to escape—in other words, practicing nonaction—makes the fear go away. For example, a cure for a fear of elevators is to ride on an elevator, carefully guided into calmness with the support of a therapist. The phobic person may feel intense anxiety at first, but nature takes its course. She feels the movement, senses herself within the small enclosure, and experiences that nothing catastrophic actually happens. Aligning with the true nature of riding the elevator causes the fear to subside. You can apply a nonaction method, using meditation, to working with your bipolar disorder, in order to help yourself naturally balance the ups and downs.

Exercise 1.3   Wu Wei: Let It Be and Accept What Is

Take a moment to sit quietly. Set your watch for two minutes and sit down in a comfortable place. Turn your attention to what you are feeling right now. Are you happy, sad, depressed, or elated? Just notice what you feel, without labeling the experience as good or bad. We all have a tendency to try to change something, often before we know what it is. So, you may find yourself trying to feel something different. Instead, simply sit quietly right now, without changing anything. Pay close attention to what you are feeling in each passing moment. The ability to notice what you are feeling, just as it is, will be a helpful skill for attuning to your energy and then being able to work with it.

You may be surprised that as you sit quietly now, paying attention to what you feel without trying to change it, you feel change happening naturally. The very act of observing adds something different to your usual experience. You might find that an uncomfortable feeling eases or a calm feeling deepens. The way of wu wei, or letting be, is a powerful method for bringing about a change naturally and almost effortlessly. We will work with wu wei later in the book, so don't worry if you find this difficult to do right now. Remember that the journey of a thousand miles begins with one step.

Yin and Yang: The Theory of Opposites

The Tao is the source, undifferentiated and empty. From this endless void, activity and inactivity arose, forming a circle of light and a circle of dark. Together, these interactions of activity and inactivity led to the universe, with its dual nature, and a continual interaction of opposites represented by the familiar symbol of yin and yang (figure 1.1). Yin and yang are the natural forces of the universe. Yin is inactive, soft, feminine, dark, and low, while yang is active, hard, masculine, bright, and high. Even though these forces can be contradictory, when in balance, they complement each other. So, as your bipolar disorder is expressed as energy, it is manifested as opposites in energy. Through awareness of yin and yang, the lows and highs in your energy, you will come to know your energy and thereby get in touch with the Tao of your bipolar disorder to foster change.

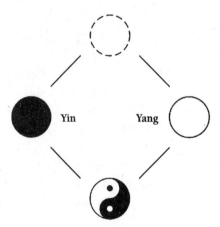

Figure 1.1

Opposites are the manifestation of the Tao in the world. They mutually produce each other as polarities that are part of the fabric of existence. They are how we know things in the world. In fact, opposites are built into our perceptual processes. Contrast is essential for distinguishing things, because we notice differences. For example, you would have difficulty discerning spatial relationships without opposites. How could you recognize "up" if there were no "down"? Or what is far without near? And understanding time also would become difficult without the conception of earlier and later. If you were always manic, you would have difficulty recognizing it. Through difference, you know yourself and your world.

As a person who has experienced strong mood swings, you probably possess an intuitive understanding of the theory of opposites, having felt conflicting forces as they pushed and pulled you in divergent directions. You have lived through fluctuations and variations, feeling firsthand the power of change in your life. By learning how to attune to the opposites and use their forces for your benefit, you will discover your Tao. Paradoxically, you start by becoming aware of yourself wherever you are, in *this* moment, even if you are in the midst of a strong mood. Your path to a dynamic balance, in tune with the Tao, your inner nature, begins where you are. And by getting in touch with yourself, whatever you are feeling here and now, you initiate a small change that begins a healing process.

Exercise 1.4 Notice Opposites

Return to what you are feeling right now. Now ask yourself, *What is the opposite?* So, for example, if you are feeling a little depressed, what is the opposite feeling? Is it happy, energized? Visualize the opposite for a moment. Recall a time when you felt, for example, happy. Now shift back to what you are feeling now. Has the experience altered a bit? Shift back and forth, sensing the interplay. According to the Tao, there is always a little of yin in yang, and some yang in yin. So, even when you are depressed, there is always some happiness to be found, even if ever so slight. Perhaps it's just a happy memory, but that sense of happiness is always potentially there as well. The relationship between the opposites is dynamic and always changing, so even a depressed mood will eventually diminish.

The Interplay of Opposites Creates Energy: Chi

From this dynamic interaction between opposite forces, energy flows. This continual flow of energy is known as *chi*. Chi is manifested in every area of living, from your inner health and vitality to the outer environment and the greater universe. The passage that follows, from the Tao Te Ching (Lao-tzu 1985, 46), expresses this idea of how matter and chi energy are connected: all coming from a single source in the Tao. Through the interplay of opposites, you get a natural, healthy flow of energy.

> All things have darkness at their back
> And strive towards the light,
> And the flowing power gives them harmony.

Chi usually flows freely in the world and in your own body, mind, and brain. As a result, everything works smoothly, as it should. But when energy is blocked, problems develop. A bipolar mood swing commits your energy strongly in one direction and makes it difficult for your chi to flow naturally. Your whole mind-brain-body system gets stuck at an overly high or low energy level. By turning your attention to your experience in meditation, a paradoxical thing happens. Energy levels in your nervous system tend to return to balance, and chi can flow. So this very simple and natural method of meditation will foster the appropriate flow of energy and redirect it for more balanced and healthier functioning. We will work extensively with chi throughout the book. But you can start the process now with this simple exercise that helps you become aware of this energy in yourself.

Exercise 1.5   Focus on Chi

There is an ancient saying: "Where the mind goes, chi flows." This exercise shows you how the flow of chi in your body is linked to your mind.

Place your hands palm up on your knees as you sit comfortably, and turn your attention now to your hands. Focus all your attention there for a few minutes. Keep all your attention focused there. Do you

19

begin to feel a little tingling in your palms or fingertips? If you have some sensations of tingling, you have experienced the flow of energy into your hands, generated by turning your attention there. You will use your attention in meditation to help moderate the flow of your energy to find better balance.

Working with Change

An ancient Chinese text, The Book of Changes (I Ching) is devoted to theories about how change occurs. There are three kinds of change— small to large, cyclical, and developmental—and as you understand them, you will better understand your mood changes. In fact, you will probably recognize your own experience in these types of change. In part 3, we will incorporate all three types of change processes to help you ease the symptoms of your bipolar disorder.

From Small to Large Change

Change begins small, almost unnoticeably. But as things go through their transformations, changes multiply exponentially, with enormous results. The I Ching points out that even heaven and earth began small and evolved over eons of time to become the complex universe of today. As you practice meditation to deal with your moods, you may not notice much change at first. But from meditative practice over time, dramatic change can take place in your lifestyle, emotions, thoughts, and cycles. A greater perspective becomes possible from the mountain peak you will reach as you journey through your life.

Exercise 1.6   Contemplate Change from Small to Large

Imagine that you throw a pebble into a pond. Can you visualize the ripples that spread out from the center through the whole pond?

From just one small pebble, the whole pond is filled with ripples. Similarly, making one small change in your own routines can send healing ripples through your whole life. Beginning now, with this quiet moment of contemplation, you can imagine that the small changes you will make as you read through this book and try the exercises can send ripples through your life in positive directions.

Cyclical Change

Another kind of change is *cyclical transformation*: one thing changes into another but eventually is restored. An example of cyclical change is the seasons, in which summer inevitably becomes fall and then winter, spring, and summer again. Bipolarity takes a cyclical form, moving from low energy, with its feelings of depression, to mania, with its high energy and elation, and then around again. You can get to know your cycles, which will help you to better predict, attune, respond, and redirect for a more balanced flow.

Exercise 1.7   Contemplate Cyclical Change

Take a few moments to think about your bipolar cycles. In later chapters, you will chart the cycles so that you can get to know them well. But for now, simply think about your ups and downs. Do they correspond with a season, or are they more frequent, such as monthly, weekly, or even daily? As you contemplate, don't judge whether they are good or bad; simply observe the timing and rhythm of your cycles.

Developmental Change

A third type of change is *progressive development*. Transformation takes place a little at a time. Each change contains the previous state, always moving forward. A life span is a good example of progressive development. The progression of your bipolar disorder as you get older is another form. Each stage of development is linked to the former one. You might not notice the changes that occur day by day, but over a longer period, change becomes easier to detect, as in the obvious transformation from childhood to adulthood. Bipolar disorder also has a progressive development. The length and intensity of cycles will change as you go through the years. Sometimes, a severe cycle can influence the next swing you have. Even if you don't notice the gradual progression, you can learn to recognize changes by thinking back on your first bipolar episode and comparing it to how you feel now. Understanding how bipolar disorder progresses over time will help you to intervene.

Exercise 1.8 Contemplate Developmental Change

Now, think about the progression of your bipolar disorder throughout your life. When did you first notice the shifts in moods? How has the disorder progressed through the years? Have you seen times when it was worse and then better? Make note of your mood-swing patterns over time.

After making some notes, fill in the following chart of the developmental changes of your mood swings over time (figure 1.2). Indicate either depression or mania with a vertical line at each five-year increment above the midline if you were manic, below the midline if you were depressed, or at the midline if you had no significant mood swings.

Do you see the moods swings becoming larger or more frequent? Or perhaps there has been more of one mood as you've gotten older?

You can create your own variation of this chart to observe a single year by making a line for each month. Or perhaps make your lines in one-year increments. Look for patterns and trends. All of this information will help you to get to know the Tao of your bipolar disorder as it has changed throughout your life.

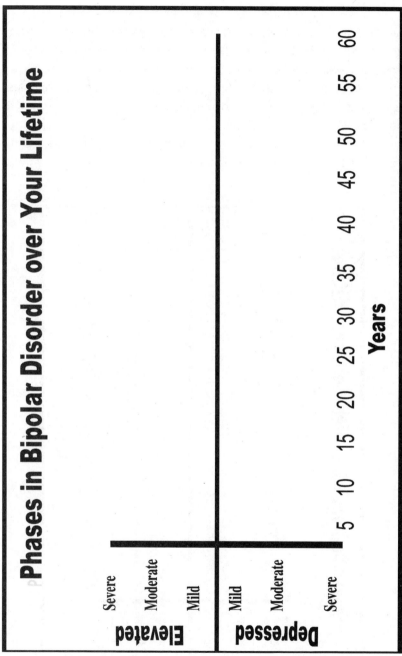

Figure 1.2

Figure 1.3 is a chart from a client named James. His first symptoms appeared suddenly, when he was twenty years old, with a strong elevation in mood followed by a severe depression and another upswing over a five-year period. He was hospitalized and put on medication, after which his swings became less frequent and less severe. He came to see us in his midforties to try to prevent another depression, since the medication didn't seem to be completely stopping his cycles. His work with meditation helped him to find a comfortable balance and lead a productive life.

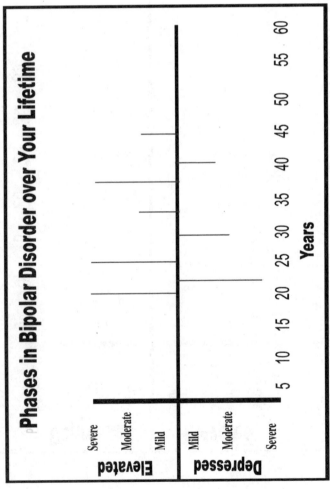

Figure 1.3

Conclusion

Everything, including your bipolar disorder, has an inner nature, with a corresponding way that you can follow that's in accord with it. There is an effortless way to return to a healthy nature when it has been lost. Meditation guides you on a path that you can follow so that you can attune to what you are experiencing moment by moment. Through non-action while being in touch and aware, you set in motion a process for a better life, one of health, harmony, and fulfillment.

By completing the exercises in this book, you will learn how to shift your energy toward balance. We will enlist all three types of change—small to large, cyclical, and developmental—effortlessly and naturally. You will begin with the small changes. You can stop a mood before it spins out of control, by becoming mindfully aware of the early signs of what you are actually doing and feeling. You will discover the forces that are at work and uncover the natural tendencies as they begin to build momentum. By becoming aware of your energy, just as it is, you gain a new kind of control. You will get to know your cycles from the inside and, through the awareness you develop, be able to moderate them. And you will be able to intervene in the development of your mood swings over time. From the wisdom you gain, you will regain control, learn how to use your energy wisely, and guide your life in more positive directions.

We hope these ideas have inspired you to look at yourself and your problems a little differently, through the lens of the Tao, wu wei, yin and yang, chi, and change. The exercises are a first glimpse of a new approach to working with your bipolar symptoms. The next chapter will help you to learn more about your bipolar disorder in ways that will help you.

Chapter 2

All about Bipolar Disorder

The more you know about your bipolar disorder, the better able you will be to cope with it and make the changes that are most helpful. This chapter informs you about bipolar disorder and mood problems using the latest scientific information. As you read, you will gain a better understanding of what you may be experiencing. You will learn about the different categories of bipolar disorder and the prominent theories as they were formulated through history, and see how bipolar disorder alters your brain structures and functions. With all of this information, combined with a description of the psychological symptoms, you will begin your meditation, armed with the key information you need to start on your path to change.

What Is Known about Bipolar Disorder, East and West

Bipolar disorder affects about one in every twenty-two people, or approximately 4.5 percent of the population (Merikangas et al. 2007), so it's not as uncommon as you might think. It is classified by the National Institute of Mental Health (NIMH 2012) as a brain disorder with strong shifts of mood, energy, and activity that get in the way of daily life. Work, school, and interpersonal relationships can suffer severe consequences from the symptoms of bipolar disorder.

From the Western, scientific perspective, bipolar disorder correlates with irregularities in the emotion centers of the brain, making emotional reactions more intense than normal. In addition, the parts of the brain that typically are involved in controlling or monitoring strong emotions tend to be smaller and less activated, so your ability to regulate your moodiness may be diminished.

Bipolar disorder is distinguished from simple moodiness. If, every day or in a regular pattern, your life sometimes seems awfully gloomy and other times extremely bright, you probably suffer from moodiness. But if your moods interfere with your life or the lives of those you care about, this may be due to symptoms of one of the forms of bipolar disorder.

The Taoist theory of bipolar disorder is that it's an energy problem, wherein energy may be blocked, stagnant, excessive, or weak. The common thread that runs through healing practices of the East is to correct these energy conditions by working directly with them. "Protecting and strengthening the right qi [chi, or energy] should be the basic principle behind all methods of health care" (Ming 2001, 283). Diagnosis of bipolar disorder involves determining the energy patterns that are preventing the normal flow.

How do these two theories of bipolar as a brain disorder and an energy disorder come together? We find the integration in the brain itself. The brain is made up of one hundred billion *neurons* that interact together to form pathways of activations and deactivations that correlate closely with what you think, feel, and do. And what are these activations and deactivations? They are electrical signals: *energy*! East meets West right there in your own nervous system!

Meditation affects the flow of energy in the brain, altering the on-off electrical signals that bring a better balance to your moods. These signals are dynamic and capable of enhancing the flow of energy or diminishing it as needed. Chapter 3 explains exactly how this happens and the research that supports it. As you meditate, you will alter the flow of energy in your nervous system to help you regulate your emotions and moods. The result is that you gain better self-control in general, along with more balanced moods.

Early Discoveries

Sometimes, understanding the past can help to clarify the present. You are not alone in your suffering. People have suffered from bipolar disorder for millennia. The modern theories of bipolar disorder derive from a fascinating showcase of classical wisdom about mental conditions, from the West as well as the East. And we learn more as time passes.

Ancient References to Bipolar Disorder

The brain aspect of the modern model derives from classical sources. The medical papyri of Egypt, such as the Ebers Papyrus, seem to mention depression and allude to the presence of bipolar disorder. Later, a clear statement by Hippocrates of Greece, the father of Western medicine (460 to 375 BCE), recognized the key role of the brain in bringing about our many moods. He said, "The people ought to know that the brain is the sole provider of pleasures and joys, laughter and jests, sadness and worry, as well as dysphoria and crying" (quoted in Post and Leverich 2008, 3).

Bipolar disorder was also observed thousands of years ago in the East. It was described in *The Medical Classic of the Yellow Emperor*, a medical text that formed the early basis for Chinese medicine, just as Hippocrates's work formed the early foundation for Western medicine. Scholars aren't sure exactly when *The Medical Classic of the Yellow Emperor* was written, but they date it somewhere between the third and first centuries BCE. This important book is filled with healing methods for many common problems, including bipolar disorder. A section about diseases is devoted to a condition that sounds like bipolar mood swings. It states, "When mania begins, the patient is sad first. Then he is exultant, irascible, and liable to fear" (Ming 2001, 212). The book describes other bipolar symptoms you may have experienced, such as not sleeping or eating well, being overly self-assertive and eloquent, and sometimes hallucinating. Treatments involve balancing the chi using meditation and acupuncture.

Development of the Bipolar Diagnosis

Western doctors have contributed greatly to our understanding of bipolar disorder. The circularity of bipolar disorder was recognized in 1851 by the French psychiatrist Jean-Pierre Falret (1784 to 1870), who observed that patients underwent a cyclical change from mania to melancholy throughout their lives.

Emil Kraepelin (1856 to 1926) was a German psychiatrist who made many observations for diagnosis that we still consider accurate and useful today, even though some of his ideas had to be corrected. He named bipolar disorder "manic depression" in 1921, characterizing its dual nature and distinguishing it from schizophrenia, with which it had previously been confused. Patients exhibited hallucinations and delusions during intense episodes, so doctors diagnosed them as psychotic. This misdiagnosis still occurs at times today. The distinction is an important one that strongly affects how you should be treated.

Kraepelin devised a helpful method of charting the cycles. We encourage you to keep an ongoing chart of your mood shifts to help you become more aware. Later in this chapter, you will find a method for charting that has been drawn from Kraepelin.

In modern times, Kraepelin's terminology has been refined. The term "manic depression" expresses Kraepelin's belief that at its root, mania is a form of depression. The euphoria, he believed, resulted from denial of depression. This belief is now considered incorrect. Mania is not just a consequence; it coexists with depression in the bipolar condition, with the potential of being a state in itself. This understanding of its true dual nature led to the renaming of the condition as "bipolar disorder," clearly distinguishing it from *monopolar disorders* such as depression.

Kraepelin recognized that even though he observed manic and depressive cycles in all his manic-depressive patients, each person had a unique variation. We have observed this too: all our bipolar clients have been talented and creative individuals, with their own rhythms and patterns. We have deep respect for the individuality of our clients. This book helps you to make your creative nature work for you.

The First Medication for Bipolar Disorder

The next leap forward came with the discovery of the stabilizing influence of lithium carbonate on mood, by the Australian psychiatrist John Cade (1912 to 1980) in 1948. The way he first came upon the idea is a good illustration of how, sometimes, positive outcomes emerge from something negative. Cade was captured as a prisoner of war during World War II. During his time in prison, he observed that when some of his fellow prisoners exhibited mood swings, their symptoms lessened after they urinated. This gave him the idea that something in their urine might be involved. After his release, he did careful research until he isolated lithium as a key element for correcting the symptoms. But there were problems with getting lithium patented for manufacture as a drug. First, lithium salts are a naturally occurring substance, so lithium carbonate could not be patented. In addition, long-term experiments needed to be done before the drug could be approved. As a result, lithium wasn't introduced in the United States as a treatment for bipolar disorder until 1970. During the 1940s, electroshock therapy, lobotomy, and other physical methods were the treatments for disorders. Cade's discovery helped to shift the emphasis from those extreme treatments toward medication, another positive outcome. Today, more work has been done to develop new medications, along with the recognition that stress reduction and different types of psychotherapy are also effective treatments, as later chapters will discuss. But lithium is still the gold standard for mania.

The Bipolar Spectrum of Moods

You have probably experienced a broad range in your moods in that they fluctuate in a cyclical pattern from low to high, and back again. These variations make sense because the bipolar condition is a spectrum. The bipolar spectrum covers a range in intensity and quality of mood: a deep level of depression, *dysthymia* (low-grade depression), *euthymia* (normal mood), *hypomania* (mild elation), and mania. These are not like the normal ups and downs of emotion. Instead, the mood change can be dramatic and passionate, occurring very quickly or building slowly over time, leading to thoughts, feelings, and behaviors that may be difficult to manage. You have probably felt strong changes in the level of energy that accompanies these different moods.

Mania

Kevin was a graduate student who had finals coming up. He felt a surge of positive energy, so instead of spending his time quietly studying as he usually did, he decided to go out on the town with his brother for some excitement. He and his brother ended up reminiscing over old times and barhopping all night. He continued to drink and party with different groups of friends for more than a week. Later, when he came down from his elated mood, he told us that he had performed poorly on his exams: "I knew I should study, but I just had too much energy to sit still!"

Mania is defined by the *Diagnostic and Statistical Manual of Mental Disorders* (DSM-IV-TR), published by the American Psychiatric Association (APA 2000), as a distinct period of a euphoric or irritable mood. This "high" is sustained for at least a week, and includes three or more other symptoms, such as grandiosity, agitation, decreased need for sleep, continuous talking, or involvement in pleasurable or risky activities like spending money, taking drugs, gambling, or promiscuity, all with highly negative consequences. Hypomania is a low-grade mood elevation, with feelings of happiness and extra energy that often include irritability.

Depression

June just couldn't bring herself to attend her three-year-old niece's birthday party. She knew she should be shopping for presents as she had done last year, but she didn't feel like doing anything. But then, late at night, she ruminated about how terrible she felt and worried that she was missing out. She told us, "I don't feel excited like I used to, even though I know how precious this time with my little niece is. I feel sad and guilty about it, but I just don't have the energy."

Depression is at the other end of the spectrum from mania and is defined by the *DSM-IV-TR* (APA 2000) as a loss of interest or pleasure. A major depressive episode lasts for at least two weeks and includes four other symptoms, such as changes in weight, appetite, and/or sleep patterns; lowered energy; feelings of guilt and worthlessness; slowed thinking; difficulty concentrating and making decisions; and thoughts about death and suicide. Dysthymia is a low-grade depression, with less-severe symptoms.

Bipolar individuals also have periods of normal mood, or euthymia. So, you probably have times when you are stable and steady, and this potential is always there. Of course, this stability is an individual balance.

Our client Judy had been diagnosed with bipolar disorder when she was in her twenties. She saw many therapists over the years. But when the treatments encouraged her to calm her mania, she protested. As she put it, "These therapists tried to get me to be something I'm not: blah and boring." And yet, she wanted to change her extreme moods, because they interfered with her music. Judy was a creative musician who didn't want to be ordinary. She meditated to become aware of her Tao, her individual way, and discovered a unique balance that wasn't too extreme but allowed her to express herself fully during performances. The methods in this book, along with the other treatments you may be using, are all meant to help you to discover your individual balance and keep from lapsing into harmful extremes.

Eastern View: Interplay of Opposites

Recall that bipolar disorder follows the flowing interplay between yin and yang. In the lows are the seeds of the highs and vice versa, as pictured in the yin-yang symbol, where a small, dark circle is found in the light half, and a small, light circle is there in the dark half (see figure 2.1).

Figure 2.1

You might not think you could possibly find anything positive about your depression. But if you apply Taoist theory, you know that even in the darkest depression, there must be some positive potential.

Our client Jeremy learned to find value in his depressed mood. He was a painter who struggled with making his work meaningful. As he began to meditate on his emotions, he came to recognize that when he was depressed, he had deep insights about the struggles of life. He learned to channel his depression into his paintings so that his work communicated the "angst" of the human condition. Over time, he became known as a painter of depth and intensity. He told us that he could now be grateful for what he had learned to express during his depression. As he came to accept his feelings, their severity lessened, and he found a better balance.

Western Categories of Bipolar

Bipolar disorder is a personal experience with consistent characteristics and individual differences, but it has been separated into three fundamental categories: bipolar I, bipolar II, and cyclothymia. Some people also have mixed states that combine some of these categories. View these categories as guidelines rather than fixed entities. You may move from one category to another. You might even have periods without symptoms, especially as you find more balance in your life.

Bipolar I

Bipolar I is a condition with a cycle that displays definite symptoms. It is the most severe of the categories, and includes both manic and depressive episodes as part of a cycle that usually recurs. The cycle may cover days, weeks, or months, depending on the individual pattern.

Bipolar I is diagnosed when at least one episode of mania has taken place that could not have been due to a reaction to drugs, medication, alcohol, or something physical. The mood state may include delusions and hallucinations, whether the mood is elation or depression. *Delusions* are beliefs that are not correlated with logic, reasoning, culture, or religion. *Hallucinations* are perceptions of people, objects, or events that have no basis in reality. Sometimes, *psychosis* emerges, which refers to a state of functioning that is out of touch with reality. In the bipolar I category, you may have self-perceptions of grandiosity, manifest great energy, feel extremely elated or excited, talk a lot, and have many thought associations during manic episodes. All of these symptoms are quite out of proportion to reality. You probably also experience a loss of good judgment, along with a wish to spend money without appropriate restraint. You might engage in impulsive behavior with strong emotionality or perhaps, instead, feel a compelling need to engage in behavior that's inappropriately narrow in goal directedness, such as continuously walking in a circle. In youth and adolescent forms of mania, the mood may be expressed as irritability, impatience, or anger. The sleep cycle is disturbed, with daily periods of only a few hours of sleep or no sleep at all.

Mixed states, sometimes called *agitated depression*, involve a simultaneous combination of depression and mania. People who have mixed states might shift from one state to another. So, you might start crying when you feel manic, or find your thoughts racing even though you feel depressed. In extreme cases, suicidal thoughts might occur as well, which can lead to life-threatening actions. Thus, the condition must be attended to immediately and responsibly. If you feel so depressed that you begin thinking about suicide, be sure to tell someone who cares, and immediately seek professional help to protect your life.

Bipolar II

If you are in this category, your symptoms tend more toward depression. You may not have needed hospitalization for the symptoms of your moods, because if you are diagnosed with *bipolar II*, you haven't lost touch with reality during episodes, as in bipolar I. The manic episodes for bipolar II sufferers, known as "hypomania," are not as extreme as for those who are diagnosed with bipolar I, and there is less mania, either for shorter periods or with less intensity. The depression part of the cycle tends to be more dominant than the manic part. Since depression can be deep and long lasting, bipolar II may feel very uncomfortable.

Cyclothymia

The mildest category in bipolar disorder, *cyclothymia* includes mild elation of mood, or hypomania, and mild to moderately depressed mood cycles that keep shifting and changing. The symptoms are not severe enough for a bipolar I or II diagnosis, even though they share the pattern of shifting moods and energy levels. The symptoms must endure for a minimum of two years to be categorized as cyclothymic, so a short period of moodiness wouldn't result in a cyclothymia diagnosis. Typically, people who have been diagnosed with cyclothymia lasting for at least two years tend to be less likely to develop a full bipolar episode as described in the previous bipolar I and II sections.

Creating a Mood Chart

The meditation methods taught in part 2 will give you an experiential way to keep track of your mood changes. But you can also add a tried-and-true Western method of charting to observe your rhythms and patterns by recording them as they happen. Figure 2.2 is a chart, drawn from the historical method of Kraepelin, for you to fill out. It guides you in noting the observable shifts in mood and energy as they occur in real time. When combined with Eastern meditations, these methods from the West will give you a deeper and clearer understanding so that you can help yourself.

Fill out this chart similarly to the developmental chart (figure 1.2) in chapter 1. In addition, make note of sensations, thoughts, or feelings that correspond with the chart for that day. You can simply note a word or phrase, or add more descriptions in a separate journal if you prefer. Over time, the chart will reveal patterns and experiences that you may not have noticed before. Add your own creative descriptions to personalize the chart with your Tao.

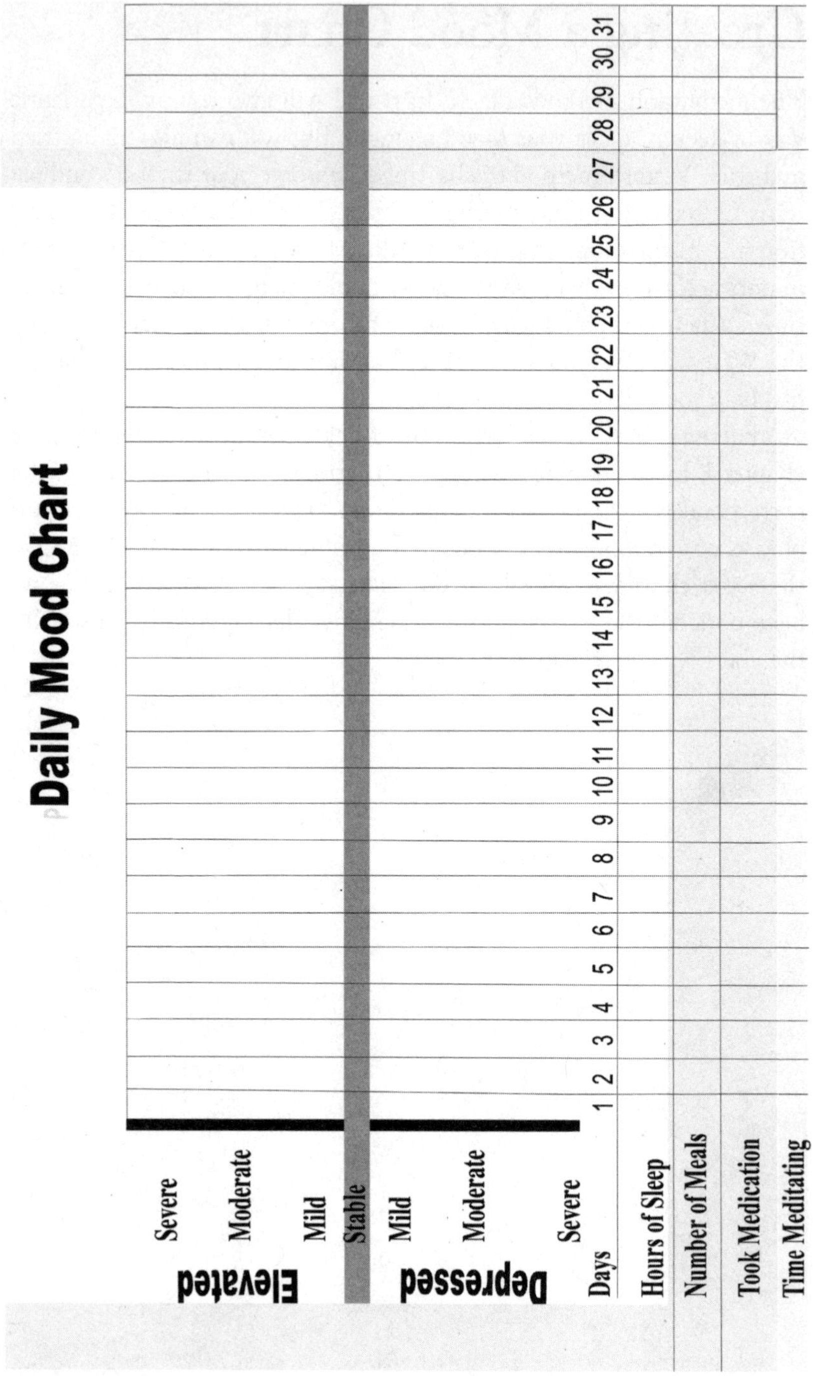

Daily Mood Chart

		Days	1	2	3	4	5	6	7	8	9	10	11	12	13	14	15	16	17	18	19	20	21	22	23	24	25	26	27	28	29	30	31
Elevated	Severe																																
	Moderate																																
	Mild																																
	Stable																																
Depressed	Mild																																
	Moderate																																
	Severe																																
		Hours of Sleep																																
		Number of Meals																																
		Took Medication																																
		Time Meditating																																

Figure 2.2

Bipolar Disorder and the Brain

Often when we explain bipolar and the brain to clients, they find the terminology a little confusing, so they may miss the main points. Therefore, before we explain how bipolar disorder affects your brain, we offer you a brief tour through the limbic system, which is a collection of many different areas that are involved in the regulation of emotions and moods in the brain. Knowing a bit about these areas will also help you to understand how meditation can affect your brain and help to make you feel better. You will be able to recognize what your nervous system needs, and thereby practice the meditations that will help you the most.

Moods Involve a Changing Network Throughout the Brain

Emotions and moods correlate with activity in the limbic system of the brain. The limbic system involves a network of structures from the lower-brain areas, which control basic body functions, all the way up to the thinking part of the brain, known as the *cortex*. What this means is that when you are feeling an emotion, the structures in the limbic system are set in motion and send signals all around your brain. This high connectivity helps to explain why emotions and moods are so important to us.

Here's how the limbic system works: Imagine for a moment that someone you love has entered the room. A part of your thinking cortex in the *temporal lobe* recognizes the face of this person and sends a message to your limbic system, specifically to an almond-shaped organ called the *amygdala*. The amygdala is involved in the processing and storage of emotional events. It becomes more activated when something is emotionally significant to you and signals that this is someone you care about. The amygdala is often considered the gateway to the limbic system, and its activation stimulates memories of your loved one in a memory area of the limbic system called the *hippocampus*. The signal passes through the *thalamus*, a gateway from the senses, and is regulated by the hypothalamus, which produces hormones. All of these limbic-system areas are located deep inside your brain. They deliver signals to your *peripheral nervous system* that reach throughout your body. The part of the peripheral nervous system that spurs you to action is the *sympathetic nervous system*. It is triggered, causing your heart rate to increase, bronchi to dilate, and even your pupils to enlarge. The result of all these complicated signals and activations is that you feel happy to see this person and walk directly over to extend a warm hug.

By contrast, if a burglar were to enter the room, your amygdala would register danger. A threat signal is passed quickly through the thalamus and hypothalamus, triggering a fear reaction in your peripheral nervous system. We will describe the details of this fear-stress system in chapter 8, on stress. Your sympathetic nervous system reacts immediately, prompting you to take action. The result of all these signals and activations is that you might shout for help, or run to the phone and call the police.

This limbic-system activity will show up on a brain scan, such as *positron-emission tomography* (PET) or *functional magnetic imaging* (fMRI). Brain scans measure the parts of the brain that become more active when you do, think, or feel something.

Understand Your Symptoms by Learning How Bipolar Affects Your Brain

If you have been diagnosed with bipolar disorder, you are likely to have irregularities in the natural limbic-system processes described previously. These findings may help to explain why your emotional moods feel so compelling. There is no final word on how bipolar disorder changes the limbic system, but here are some of the emerging trends.

Studies of people with bipolar disorder have found an enlargement in the amygdala (Strakowski et al. 1999). Since bipolar disorder is usually accompanied by stronger-than-normal moods, these results are not surprising. Thus, in our previous examples, you would tend to have stronger and more-extreme reactions. These research findings tell you that any way you can normalize your limbic system is likely to be helpful. Research shows that meditation calms an overactivated limbic system in a number of different ways. Chapter 3 provides the research and explains how meditation helps change the brain.

Another finding that seems to be consistent across many studies is that the face-recognition ability in the temporal lobes and the thinking and control areas of the brain in your *frontal cortices* tend to be smaller. Researchers found smaller temporal-lobe volumes on both the left and right sides in patients with bipolar disorder than in people who were not bipolar (El-Badri et al. 2006). The temporal lobes are closely linked to the limbic system, making them strongly involved in emotion. They regulate your ability to recognize and react to emotions in other people's faces. The smaller volumes in your temporal lobe lead to a tendency to misinterpret other people's emotions (Derntl et al. 2009).

Having a smaller volume in part of the thinking areas of the brain may contribute to the difficulty you have in controlling your moods. Another study (Bremner 2005) found smaller volumes in the *prefrontal cortex* among people with bipolar disorder. This also makes sense, since the prefrontal cortex is used when people are performing *executive functions* like planning, working toward a goal, or making decisions. The smaller volumes in the prefrontal cortex help to explain why it feels so difficult to plan and do things when you are feeling depressed. And smaller prefrontal-cortex volumes may also explain poor decision making and difficulty making sensible plans when you are manic. Regular meditation practice enhances executive functioning, making it easier to make decisions, carry out plans, and follow through on goals. Meditation has been shown to thicken the attentional areas located in the prefrontal cortex (Lazar et al. 2005). So meditating may help to correct the smaller volumes in the prefrontal cortex, as chapter 3 will describe. And you will see improved thinking after regular meditation, which will help moderate your moods.

Here is another bit of compelling evidence that helps to explain some of your bipolar reactions. The *cingulate gyrus*, a deep part of the cerebral cortex, is located close to the limbic system. It connects the limbic system structures to higher parts of the frontal lobes, and sends messages between your emotional limbic system and key parts of your thinking cortex. The cingulate gyrus becomes activated when you try to control your emotions and moods. Thus, the cingulate gyrus is involved in *self-regulation*, a term that psychologists use to describe how you calm yourself down when you are feeling angry and irritable, or cheer yourself up when you are feeling sad and sluggish. Being able to self-regulate is a very important skill, and meditation has been found to help people regulate their emotions (Tang et al. 2009). Bipolar patients were found to have lower density in the cingulate gyrus, compared to people without bipolar disorder (Benes, Vincent, and Todtenkopf 2001). These findings may explain why you have difficulty regulating your emotions. Chapter 3 will present the meditation research that shows that meditating helps you regulate your emotions. So you have good reasons for trying meditation to help you with your moods.

Treatments

A diagnosis of bipolar warrants both prescriptions for medication and treatment of behavioral symptoms. Because bipolar is classified as a brain disorder, medications that alter the brain have been and continue to be a viable treatment for bipolar disorder. A variety of medications are used, some of which might seem to be suited to other problems. Although you can also exert a lot of influence on your own condition, medication is an important resource. The methods included in this book are not substitutes for correct use of pharmacology, which is directed by your doctor or psychopharmacologist. But using the methods presented in this book in conjunction with medication improves your chances of good management and recovery from dark moments in your bipolar condition. If medication has been prescribed for you, we strongly urge you to take it, and some of the meditations offered in this book will make it easier for you to remember to do so.

However, medications alone do not give most people relief from suffering. In fact, according to the National Institute of Mental Health, medication combined with some kind of therapeutic intervention works best for the treatment of people of all ages who are depressed, with early evidence presented in the 1990s and continuing to build over decades (Antonuccio, Danton, and DeNelsky 1995; Kennard et al. 2008). A comprehensive study of bipolar disorder has not been conducted, but our clinical experience over many years in working with bipolar clients who are also taking medication has shown us that adding meditation can improve the effectiveness of treatment overall. Meditation has its own body of research showing how it will complement your pharmacological treatments in a number of important ways. First, meditation has been found to stabilize the nervous system (Dillbeck et al. 1986). It also has dual effects, simultaneously bringing relaxation and alertness (Hugdahl 1996; Lazar et al. 2005). In addition, meditation helps to regulate emotions (Tang et al. 2009). Chapter 3 will give you the details of this research.

Conclusion

Bipolar disorder involves a dynamic, changing shift in moods that interferes with your life. Western and Eastern treatments work well together to improve symptoms. Medications help to alter your brain chemistry for the better. Meditation changes your brain balance, offering stability to the limbic system and increased activation to the *attentional system*, a fundamental part of the thinking brain. So, by meditating, you can help to correct some of the irregularities in your brain. In addition, you become more alert and aware, thereby improving your thinking abilities, which are so important in helping you to regulate your moods.

This book gives you methods that help you affect your emotional state with meditation, not just medication. The best path is the middle one, including some yin and some yang on the spectrum. The positive effects you bring about are lasting and will contribute to a meaningful life.

Now that you have some background on your bipolar disorder, you will find chapter 3 helpful for learning how you can change your brain by what you do and how meditation can help you bring your brain and nervous system into better balance.

How Meditation Can Change Your Brain

Imagine for a moment what an explorer might have felt in coming across a new land that no one knew existed. What an exciting moment in history, to find an undiscovered continent! We are in the midst of a similar moment in history, when the undiscovered territory is the human brain, with its exciting promise for human potential. Only recently have researchers begun to realize that your brain is capable of reorganizing many of its neural pathways, connections, and functions throughout life. And these changes can be brought about through your own life experiences, including the treatments you use for your bipolar disorder. You probably know that your medications alter your brain, but you may not have realized that meditation can change the functions and structures of your brain in helpful ways too!

Meditation is one of the tools this book teaches for altering the course of your bipolar disorder. Keep in mind that meditation will work best when you practice it while taking your medication. By combining meditation with Western treatments, you will gain more options, increasing the effectiveness of both approaches. Meditation will give you beneficial tools to help you help yourself.

This chapter will give you a basic understanding of how you may be able to affect the typical brain patterns of bipolar disorder using meditation. Connections within the brain can alter throughout life, allowing learning and behavior to change at any time. You will learn what specific areas of the brain are affected when you have bipolar disorder and how meditation influences them for the better. And you will see how these changes tend to improve your ability to moderate your moods to overcome the problems you have from bipolar disorder.

Bipolar Disorder Arises at the Connections between Neurons

Recent research on bipolar disorder supports a new view about how this condition comes about. Bipolar disorder arises from how the neurons in the brain communicate with each other. According to one research group, bipolar illness can be conceptualized as a disorder of the *synapses* (small space between neurons) and circuits, rather than as only deficits or excesses of neurotransmitters (Schloesser et al. 2008). Usually the neurons can flexibly form new connections between them (an ability known as *neuroplasticity*). These researchers found that plasticity between neurons in people who have bipolar disorder does not occur as it does in those who don't have bipolar disorder. Their research suggests that by addressing neuroplasticity itself, you may be able to alter some of the brain patterns in depression and mania. Thus, it will be helpful for you to gain a deeper understanding of neuroplasticity and learn ways to foster better communication between neurons.

These findings are new and hopeful. Neuroplasticity can occur from what you experience, what you do, and even how you use your mind. Neuronal connections are somewhat plastic, so given the right experiences, you may be able to alter your symptoms by changing the connections between neurons. Meditation can foster neuroplasticity between neurons in the areas that are important for bipolar disorder, as this chapter will describe, giving you a brain basis for applying this method. And of course, meditation will also make you feel and think better—another good reason for working with these approaches!

Neuroplasticity: How Your Brain Can Change

For decades, Western scientists believed that generally, once you have passed adolescence and reached adulthood, your brain doesn't change. But in recent years, scientific evidence from the West coincides with ancient wisdom of the East in discovering that the brain is not fixed, but actually is somewhat plastic and malleable throughout life. In fact, the brain can change at any age.

Neuroplasticity is the brain's ability to alter and grow new neural connections. This capacity for the brain to change offers a new way to help alter the patterns of bipolar symptoms by initiating change at the neuronal level. Meditation has been shown to affect the connections between neurons in areas that improve bipolar symptoms. Thus, by meditating you elicit the kinds of brain changes you need to stabilize your moods and stay in balance.

V. S. Ramachandran has performed groundbreaking research showing many ways that neural connections change and adapt (Ramachandran and Blakeslee 1999; Ramachandran 2011). For example, when people lose their sight, their other senses become sharper. You may know someone who is blind, and have noticed how acute that person's senses of touch and hearing are. This is because the vision areas of the brain become remapped for use by the other senses. Remapping occurs in many systems of the brain.

How Neuroplasticity Occurs

Neuroplasticity begins at the connections between the cells in the brain, the neurons. The system of neurons known as the *central nervous system* (CNS) extends throughout the entire body. It includes the brain, the spinal cord, the cranial nerves, and the peripheral nervous system. The neurons interlink, forming a network of electrical activity. The electrical activity in the nervous system accounts for what we think and feel. So, for example, when you are having a strong mood, there is more electrical activity in the emotional centers of the brain. Your brain has approximately one hundred billion neurons interacting with each other that are capable of making a trillion connections in a vast network of communication. So you can appreciate how complex the brain interconnections can be!

Neurons don't literally touch each other. Instead, they are separated at the synapses. Neurons communicate across the synapse by sending an electrical signal between them. When the neurons are close enough, the electrical impulse can jump directly across the synapse from one neuron to another, but when there is a larger space, chemicals known as *neurotransmitters* transmit the signal across the synapse and cause the next neuron to fire.

Psychiatric medications influence the flow of neurotransmitters by either keeping more of certain neurotransmitters in the synapse when there aren't enough or blocking the flow of those neurotransmitters when the brain is producing too many of them. In these ways, some medications make the next cell fire, while others stop the neurons from firing. The result is that the electrical signals are sent and received as they should in order to help you feel less depressed or more calm for a balanced level of energy. Thus, what medications really do is help your brain to alter the electrical signals between neurons.

Shifts in the signals between neurons can also be affected by meditation. Since meditation is the emphasis in this book, we will be addressing the influence of meditation on the brain in general and on your bipolar disorder specifically.

Hebb's Rule and LTP and LTD

When neurons fire together regularly, they begin to form stronger bonds. One of the pioneers in modern neuroscience, Donald Hebb (1949), coined the catchy phrase "Neurons that fire together wire together." For example, when you have an experience repeatedly, a network of neurons involved in that experience will fire, sending signals across their synapses. So, when you feel depressed, certain neurons become associated together and fire together. The next time your depressive cycle returns, this pattern of neurons fires together again, forming a stronger bond between those neurons. The neurons fire together repeatedly the more times you have depressive cycles, and eventually become wired together, making your depression difficult to change. What has happened at the neuronal level is called *long-term potentiation* (LTP). Many scientists now think LTP is a cellular explanation for how learning and memory take place in your brain (Cooke and Bliss 2006).

The bonds that form between neurons in LTP can also be loosened through something called *long-term depression* (LTD), a process that decreases their connections. The old expression "Use it or lose it" applies here. The bonds between neurons, if left unused, loosen and eventually let go. LTD can be helpful when you are trying to change a negative pattern. As you work with meditation, you will have new experiences that counter the effects of depression and mania. As you have more meditative experiences, you loosen the connections in the brain that make you feel moody, and forge new ones that help you to feel alert, calm, and balanced.

Neurotrophic Factors and Stress

You can see how neuroplasticity involves electrical activity between neurons. But there is one additional bit of information that will help you to understand how neuroplasticity is enhanced or inhibited. Something called *neurotrophic factor* encourages this growth of neurons. Neurotrophic factors are the family of proteins that bring about the survival, development, and growth of neurons. Neurotrophic factors promote brain plasticity. Stress blocks the release of neurotrophic factors (Duman and Monteggia 2006), whereas this release is enhanced by meditation (Hölzel et al. 2011) and your medications. There is mounting evidence that stress plays an important role in bipolar disorder. Chapter 8, on stress, will help you to counter the negative effects of stress by lowering your vulnerability to stress and relapse. Two experts on the treatment of bipolar disorder, Robert Post and Gariele Leverich (2008), hypothesize that treatment for enhancing the brain's capability to cope with stress will lessen the effect of stress on neurotrophic factors, thereby permitting natural brain plasticity to take place.

How to Enhance Neuroplasticity

Neurons have this ability to modulate the strength and structure of their synaptic connections through certain types of experiences, like deliberately focusing on something to help you remember it. You can deliberately engage in certain activities that aid in strengthening or loosening key neuronal bonds that may be influencing your bipolar symptoms. You literally change some of the connections in your brain by the ways you think and what you do. Neuroplasticity from LTP, LTD, and neurotrophic factors can be helpful in making changes in your bipolar disorder.

Researchers have investigated what kinds of experiences tend to foster neuroplasticity. They found that enriched environments stimulated more connections between neurons. When they put mice in cages filled with toys and wheels that mice enjoy, along with other mice to play with, the connections in the brains of the mice became denser and more visible. In addition, the branching out from each neuron became more complex, just as branches grow as a tree matures (Greenough, Black, and Wallace 1987). The same effect resulted when mice that had been raised in simple laboratory cages were placed into more interesting cages. This growth in new neuronal material, called *neurogenesis*, was found in all of these mice. And the part in the brain in which the growth appeared was the hippocampus (Briones, Klintsova, and Greenough 2004). The hippocampus is involved in learning and memory. The mice with the larger hippocampi performed better in learning and memory tasks.

So, what do all of these results tell you about helping to ease your mood problems? The drug treatments you may be using are one powerful way to change your brain. Medications help to rebalance the continually flowing electrical signals and chemicals in your brain at the synapses by changing the balance of neurotransmitters and thereby helping to stabilize your moods.

But there is much more that you can do. Regular practice of meditation strengthens neural pathways that support equanimity, focused attention, and calm alertness, making cognitive and emotional balance a habit. Meditation has certain kinds of explicit effects that change the brain in ways that are specifically helpful for bipolar disorder. When you use meditation along with your medication, you set a process in motion that gathers momentum in positive ways. The next section will explain how meditation can help you change your brain.

How Meditation Changes the Bipolar Brain

Meditation can help you in a number of different ways. It can calm you when you are overstimulated, add alertness and focus when you are feeling depressed, and enhance your ability to regulate your moodiness. We provide key selections from the research about these three effects of meditation. We have also written extensively about the research and applications of meditation for psychological problems in our books *Meditation for Therapists and Their Clients* (W. W. Norton and Company, 2009), *Meditation and Yoga in Psychotherapy: Techniques for Clinical Practice* (John Wiley and Sons, 2011), and *Zen Meditation in Psychotherapy: Techniques for Clinical Practice* (John Wiley and Sons, 2012). New research is ongoing.

Many of the studies cited in this chapter use the tools of neuroscience for measuring changes in the brain, such as electroencephalogram (EEG), and neuroimaging technologies, such as magnetic resonance imaging (MRI) and functional magnetic resonance imaging (fMRI), to name a few of those that are most widely used. Whenever we refer to EEG, MRI, or fMRI in the research we describe, please realize that these imaging technologies are not an exact representation, like a photograph, but they do give us patterns and tendencies that help to unlock the mysteries of the brain and how it relates to what we think, feel, and do.

The Calming Effect of Meditation

Researchers have long known that for calming the nervous system, meditation is superior to simply resting. Prolific meditation researchers Michael Dillbeck and David Orme-Johnson (1987) did a metastudy consisting of many studies, all of which showed how beneficial meditation is for calming down. When you practice meditation, you activate a relaxation response from your *parasympathetic nervous system* (the calming part of your nervous system). Thus, simply taking some time to meditate can enhance your natural ability to be calm. This capacity is built in, but we often don't know how to tap into it when we need to.

Dual Simultaneous Effects of Meditation: Relaxation and Alertness

Clearly, then, relaxation is one of the qualities that meditation can bring about. But meditation has the dual simultaneous effects of relaxation and alertness. These findings have been confirmed by fMRI and EEG studies (Hugdahl 1996). Your brain not only becomes more relaxed during meditation, but also is activated in helpful ways.

A number of recent studies have elaborated on these interesting dual effects from meditation (Lazar et al. 2005). Typically, when people are paying close attention, they are not relaxed. Instead, they tend to be physiologically aroused, and their brains and nervous systems show a corresponding stimulation. You have probably experienced this combination of alertness and tension when you had to watch the road carefully as you drove though rush-hour traffic, or if you have ever had to stand up in front of a group to give a report. By contrast, when you meditate, you tend to have a low heart rate and slow breathing, which are qualities of relaxation, while remaining highly alert and aware. You gain the ability to direct your attention to whatever is needed without being tense. Maintaining alertness without experiencing corresponding tension can prove helpful for better handling the stress and challenge of your moods with calm awareness.

The Mood-Regulating Effect of Meditation from the Frontal Lobes

If you have bipolar disorder, you may have an overactivated limbic system, which regulates emotion. You may also have smaller, underactivated parts of your frontal and temporal lobes, which results in struggles with thoughts and emotions at times. But you can turn that around by adding meditation to your treatment plan. Meditation makes real and lasting changes in the emotional and thinking centers of the brain. These changes will help you to be less controlled by your moods, giving you the power to handle your life comfortably and well. Meditation stimulates attentional areas in the frontal lobes, which are key for helping you to think more clearly and make better decisions. One fascinating study found that people who meditated regularly for around forty-five minutes a day over a number of years had thicker prefrontal cortices (areas that regulate attentiveness) than nonmeditators of the same age. In addition, the meditators had more thickness than nonmeditators in their *insula*, an area involved in awareness of internal body experiences (Lazar et al. 2005). The insula is also activated when you have social feelings of empathy, compassion, fairness, and cooperation. Greater thickness in these two areas can make it easier for you to regulate your moods and exercise better judgment in interactions with others.

The cingulate gyrus, another frontal lobe area, is also activated by meditation. Recall that the cingulate gyrus activates when people are regulating their moods and emotions. People with bipolar disorder have lower activation in this area. So, an activity that increases the activation in your cingulate gyrus will help you to have better control over your moodiness. A recent meditation study measured the physiological and brain changes of subjects before, during, and after five days of meditation training. They were compared to a control group who practiced relaxation but not meditation. The meditation group was better able to regulate their emotional reactions than the relaxation group. The neuroimaging data revealed more activity in the anterior (front) part of the cingulate gyrus from meditating subjects, which correlated with better self-regulation of their emotions than the relaxation group (Tang et al. 2009).

In a more recent study, Yi-Yuan Tang and colleagues found that structural changes in the brain had occurred from a brief meditation course. They discovered that in the meditating group, the white-matter connectivity increased between the front part of the cingulate gyrus and other structures of the brain (Tang et al. 2010). Thus, meditation might literally enhance the neural networks that help you to regulate your moods, making it easier for you to recognize and work with them.

The Mood-Moderating Effects of Meditation over Time

The many positive effects of meditation get stronger as you practice it over time. For example, one group of researchers used fMRI to show that the relaxation response that people get when meditating develops slowly. The subjects meditated for forty-five minutes, with the second brain scan showing increased effects over the first scan (Lazar et al. 2000). These results suggest that meditation is dynamic, with results increasing throughout the meditation session as the individual gradually becomes calmer over time. Based on these results, you should be patient as you work with meditation. Even though you may not feel much at first, the effects are likely to grow stronger over time. Have confidence and keep meditating!

Different Kinds of Meditation for Different Moods

Researchers have measured meditators from a number of different meditation traditions and compared the effects using EEG, MRI, and fMRI. As you know, bipolarity involves many different kinds of moods. You will need to have a variety of methods at your command to use at different points in your cycle. Logically, you know that you don't do the same thing for every situation. Water quenches your thirst but not your hunger. Similarly, with meditation, different forms have different effects. Some meditations focus your attention and sustain it on one thing. Other forms of meditation open the focus of your attention and let it change over time. And still other kinds of meditation have no focus at all but simply keep your mind clear. Each of these types of meditation will have a different effect on how you feel and think. These different types of meditation also have different effects on the brain, showing patterned combinations of brain waves measured by EEG, which vary depending on the type of meditation used.

Focus Meditation

Focus meditation involves directed concentration, such as focusing on breathing or on an image. This kind of meditation narrows your attention to a specific object of focus. This skill will be useful in overcoming unwanted thoughts by redirecting your attention in healthier ways. You can learn to direct your thoughts away from disturbing ruminations and toward more positive and hopeful thoughts. Focus meditation, such as attending to your breathing, also brings relaxation and calm, which reduces stress. Meditators who did focus meditation and were measured with EEG recorded the shorter gamma and beta waves that correlate with deliberately paying attention (Lutz et al. 2004). Thus, this form of meditation activates the attention centers of the brain.

Open-Focus Meditation

Several types of meditation are nondirected and open, such as mindfulness and compassion meditations. Here, the object of focus continually changes and is free to move, as in moment-by-moment mindfulness meditation. Attention is open and changing. Mindfulness meditation can help you to become more aware of what you are actually experiencing as it happens, which is helpful for getting to know your moods and the signs of swinging up or down. With this awareness, you will be better equipped to moderate your moods and stay in balance.

When people who were doing open-focus meditation were measured, their brains showed an increase in theta waves in the frontal and temporal-central areas of the brain, which are so crucial for regulating your emotions (Lagopoulos et al. 2009). While meditating, subjects also showed an increase in alpha waves. This makes sense, because mindfulness meditation involves paying attention but in a comfortable and natural way, just noticing what's happening as it happens. One of the concerns that bipolar people often have is whether they will retain the ability to be alert and active, as they are when feeling manic. Meditation fosters alertness, but does so in a relaxed way.

People still ask, "Why not simply sleep or rest?" Meditation is different from just relaxing. The brain waves of subjects who practiced simple relaxation did not show increased theta or alpha waves, because they were not paying attention to anything (ibid.). Theta waves correlate with relaxed attention that monitors inner experiencing and with creativity, deeply relaxed tranquility, and restful alertness. Alpha waves are associated with relaxed attention. It makes sense to find theta and alpha waves correlated with open-focus forms of meditation, where people are monitoring their ongoing experience in a relaxed and flowing way. You will find that this ability to pay attention without becoming hyperalert will help you to moderate a manic reaction while accomplishing some of the tasks that are important to you. And it will also help to moderate depression, because the relaxed attention replaces the tense rumination and judgment that accompany depression.

No-Focus Meditation

More recently, Fred Travis and Jonathan Shear (2010) have distinguished another form of meditation, known as no-focus meditation, or *automatic self-transcending meditation*, which is characterized by its absence of both focus and control or effort. Here meditators transcend their own activity, letting go to the experience. As a result, they find that they can simply respond automatically and effortlessly. The EEG associated with no-focus meditation was shown to correlate with a very intense type of alpha wave. These alpha waves tend to occur when people have relaxed attention while remaining alert without really trying to do so. And these waves accompany experiences of well-being and comfort. Practicing automatic no-focus meditation can lessen much of the discomfort you feel. As you learn to have a clear consciousness and remain centered in the present moment, free of obstructions from intruding thoughts, you are open to new possibilities.

How the Different Forms of Meditation Help with Bipolar Symptoms

Each of the different forms of meditation (focus, open-focus, and no-focus) can foster certain mental abilities, such as attention, memory, and awareness. Each form can also help you to regulate your emotions, to be steady and aware of what you feel, and to increase your overall sense of happiness. As you learn these different forms of meditation, you will sense what works best for you in different situations and for different moods.

Focus meditations that teach you how to hold your attention on one thing, such as breathing or compassion, calm the central nervous system to lower stress. Focus meditations also help you to gain better control over your attention. You will practice directing your attention away from inner rumination. Ruminating perpetuates depression, so this form of meditation will help you to feel less depressed. You will also develop ways to slow racing thoughts to help with the negative symptoms of mania.

Open-focus meditations, such as mindfulness and compassion meditations, stimulate the cingulate gyrus, the area that is involved in helping you to regulate your moods and moderate your energy. These meditations also stimulate the insula, giving a better internal body sense. Thus, you will be more in touch with yourself and more aware of what you are doing as you do it, for better mood regulation. In addition, you will learn ways to stop judging yourself, which is helpful in easing depression.

When your energy levels are extreme, such as when you are feeling elated or depressed, no-focus meditations can free your energy from being stuck at an excessively high or low level. New possibilities emerge to help ease troublesome moods as you clear away the problems that trouble your mind. And all forms of meditation enhance your feeling of well-being from a place of relaxed, centered, and balanced energy.

These are a few of the ways that the different kinds of meditations included in this book will help you to alleviate some of the symptoms of your bipolar disorder. You will learn how and when to practice these different forms of meditation in later chapters.

Conclusion

Meditation can help you make real changes in your brain. You can improve the regulation of your emotional limbic system and increase activation of parts of your thinking cortex in the frontal and temporal lobes and in the cingulate gyrus, all of which help regulate your moodiness. You can also enlist your parasympathetic nervous system to calm you when you are overactivated from a high mood, or stimulate your sympathetic nervous system to give you more energy when you feel low. All of these changes that come about from the regular practice of meditation will enlist your mind, brain, and body to work together to help you feel more stable, more alert, and better able to maintain an optimal balance of energy.

You have different meditation tools to achieve these varied changes. You can use focus, open-focus, or no-focus meditation. Although different meditations bring about different results, all of these practices will increase certain qualities, such as feelings of well-being, heightened awareness, greater relaxation, and enhanced regulation of emotions and moods. We encourage you to have confidence that the meditations in this book can help you in many ways to ease your varied moods over time. Meditation has been found to be helpful to all kinds of people who have felt depressed, anxious, irritable, and overly energized, and you, too, can share in its benefits.

Part 2

Learning Meditation

Chapter 4

Warming Up to Meditation

Meditation begins as naturally and easily as just sitting down on a cushion to experience a quiet moment. It derives from your built-in capacities to sense, perceive, and pay attention. You might not have expected that something so simple could be so beneficial, but if you have read part 1, you have seen why and how meditation unlocks the ability of your mind and brain to help you with bipolar disorder.

You learn meditation by doing it. The more you do it, the more skilled you become. In this chapter, you will learn how to get ready for meditation and hone your skills. Then you will find it easier to try the different forms of meditation offered in the chapters that follow. By practicing these exercises regularly, you share in a tradition that has enriched the lives of people around the world for centuries, while finding balance for your moods and better use of your capabilities.

A Place to Meditate

People often ask, "Where should I meditate?" The atmosphere of the place you choose can be very helpful, especially at first. Once you are well acquainted with meditation, you can do it almost anywhere. And yet, you might like having a meditative place to visit, even after you become skilled in the practice.

At first, find a quiet place to meditate. Quiet surroundings foster a quiet mind. It may be a separate room or even just a corner somewhere in your house. Set up the area with a chair or meditation cushion for sitting, or a mat or couch to lie down on. Lighting should be subdued, not too dark or too light. Some people may want to burn incense or bring in a fragrant plant. Meditation rooms are traditionally decorated tastefully but sparsely, to create an atmosphere of peaceful sanctuary. A single flower in a vase, a lone calligraphic scroll hanging on a blank wall, and pillows on a wooden floor are usually the only decorations. Keep it simple and comforting for you.

Nature can be inspirational for meditation. Meditation done outdoors in your own yard, at a park, in the woods, or perhaps in a beautiful garden can help to bring about a feeling of quiet and peace. Water can also have a calming effect. The beach, the shore of a lake, the edge of a pond, the bank of a stream, even a room with a small water fountain in it can all be possible sites for a meditation session. Most of us have enjoyed the soothing tap-tap of rain falling on the roof, and felt naturally soothed. You can use these natural tendencies to help deepen your meditative experience.

All of these settings are optional enhancements. Keep in mind that the essential component is you and your willingness to try. So choose a place to meditate where you feel at ease. Return to the same place each time for meditation. Habit and consistency help. Eventually you will find that benefits flow very naturally from your special meditation place to wherever you are. Like a gentle breeze, the spirit of meditation will permeate your world.

A Time to Meditate

Whenever we have given a lecture on meditation, people complain that their lives are far too hectic already and that they can't imagine finding any time to meditate. They are always surprised to discover that the meditative process can be set in motion in as little as one minute! How much time you devote to meditation is a very personal matter. Undoubtedly there are wasted moments in your day or evening that you can make use of. You might begin with one or two minutes a day, and work up to a half hour, but even ten minutes a day can have an effect.

Sometimes people feel frustrated or even bored with meditation. In our experience, we have found that this occurs when they are trying to meditate for too long. Endurance for meditation builds with practice. If you start with just a few minutes, you won't tend to feel bored or frustrated. But if you push yourself too hard, too fast, you are more likely to meet with such resistance. And keep in mind that the unconscious, inner mind does not function on clock time the way the conscious mind does. Sometimes your deepest meditative experience occurs in a flash. Then again, an insight may evolve over many months of meditative practice.

Meditate at least one time, nearly every day. If you are using your meditation practice to learn how to balance your moods, you should meditate several times during the day. Start from where you are, devoting the time that you can comfortably fit within your schedule, even if it's just one or two minutes at a time. But above all, meditate regularly and be faithful to your practice. If you are in a low mood, you might not feel much like meditating. But you can probably meditate for one minute or even less time. And if you do several short sessions at different times during the day, you may be pleasantly surprised as you start to feel a little better.

You will probably experience meditation when you are manic differently from when you are depressed. We offer separate chapters for each mood, with chapter 9 to moderate your downs and chapter 10 to ease your ups. You have distinct needs and capacities at different points in your cycle, so you will want to sensitively attune your practice to fit what's possible for you then. Eventually, you are likely to experience more balance, especially as your meditative practice becomes stronger.

Be gentle and patient with yourself. Everyone starts at the beginning. And in meditation, *beginner's mind*, as it is called—when you don't know what to expect and are simply open to learning—is considered valuable and even enlightened. From having seen many bipolar people learn how to meditate effectively, we believe that if you are wholehearted in your attempts, you will be able to meditate.

Finding Your Meditation Postures

Meditation is traditionally done sitting on the floor, standing, or lying down. Where and exactly how you stand, sit, or lie down is not as important as the fact that you are meditating. Once you can meditate comfortably, you will be able to extend your meditative mind into other aspects of your daily life, such as when you are moving and doing things.

Two qualities are important to develop in your meditation posture: alertness and relaxation. You may be surprised that the best way to develop them is not by trying to make yourself be that way. You will be far more successful by simply observing and noticing the reactions of your body and your breath as you are sitting, standing, or lying down. Gradually you will start to recognize when you are relaxed or alert from subtle cues like changes in your breathing rate or comfort in your body position. With practice, you will be able to deepen the experience if you want to. One of the nice benefits of meditation is that the relaxed, alert posture you develop begins to generalize into all of your activities.

We all live under the influence of gravity. When you are aligned with gravity, your posture improves to the point where you find that standing, walking, and sitting become easier, and so does meditation. When you are aligned, your muscles are more relaxed and your movements flow more easily. You will feel the difference between being aligned and unaligned as you try the exercises that follow. We encourage you to do the exercises to experience the difference for yourself. The evidence is internal: your felt sense of your body being in balance.

How can you become more aligned? Simply trying to force yourself to stand up straight will not necessarily make you more aligned, nor will it help you to meditate better. Instead, begin by paying attention to your body as it is. Then you will sense your way to your alignment with gravity. In the process, you will want to make small adjustments. This series of exercises will assist you in finding the balance and positioning that is most aligned and comfortable for sitting, standing, and lying down.

Later chapters will teach you ways to work with your breathing, but for now, simply let your breathing become light and natural. Another question people ask is whether to keep their eyes open or closed. Meditation can be done both ways. Or your eyes can remain half opened, half closed. If you are on medication that makes you dizzy or if you have troubling thoughts that bother you when you close your eyes, we advise you to keep your eyes open. But if closing your eyes feels comfortable, you may find it easier to concentrate with your eyes closed. Experiment with all three ways, and you will sense for yourself which way works best to start. Eventually you will probably use different eye positions depending on what kind of meditation you are doing. We will give specific guidance with the exercises in the book.

The Sitting Posture

Sitting is the most common meditative posture. A number of different sitting positions work well for meditating. If you are able to do so, sit comfortably, cross-legged on the floor on a cushion. If you practice yoga, you can use the full-lotus or half-lotus position if it's comfortable for you. For the purposes of therapeutic meditation, simply sitting cross-legged is all you need to do. Keep your head up with your neck comfortably straight.

Another meditation position that you might like to try is to sit in a kneeling position. Kneel down on a cushion and then sit back on your heels. Allow your back and neck to remain fairly straight, with your face pointing straight ahead.

If you prefer not to sit on the floor, use a low bench or chair. When sitting in a chair, ensure that it is well balanced with a firm seat. Sit slightly forward on the seat, with your feet planted firmly on the floor and your hands resting on your knees. You may feel as if you need more support, especially if you are taking medications, so hold on to the sides of the chair seat or chair arms as you sit.

Close your eyes fully or partially. Keep your shoulders open without hunching forward, so that your breathing passages are clear. Sometimes when people become relaxed, they slump forward. If you feel yourself leaning, gently straighten up.

You can place your hands in any one of the standard meditative positions. One way is to let your hands rest on your knees, palms down. A second way is to extend your arms so that the backs of your hands are over your knees. You may also clasp your forefinger and thumb in a circle, with the other three fingers extended. A third method is to place your hands together, with the back of one hand resting over the palm of the other and your elbows bent. Fingertips can be either together or with a

65

rounded space between them. Your body proportions will tend to make one way feel more comfortable than another. For example, if your arms are long, extending your arms over your knees usually feels natural. If your upper body is shorter, the handclasp position may feel more comfortable. Find the position that's most comfortable for you.

Exercise 4.1   Find Your Sitting Posture

If you are having an upswing in mood, you may find it difficult to sit still. And if you are experiencing a downswing, you may have trouble feeling comfortable. This exercise helps you discover a way to sit that puts you at ease. You can find a sitting position that feels almost effortless, aligned with gravity.

Sit down in one of the positions described previously. Rock forward very slightly and then rock slightly back. Rock forward and then back several times—not so far as to lose your balance, just enough to feel a gentle shift. Feel the motion as you move; experience how you pass through a natural balance point at the center, where your muscles feel more relaxed. Continue to sway for several minutes, noticing as you pass through the balance point in the center. When you feel that you can recognize it, gently rock back to that center point and remain there for a moment. Next, rock sideways: left and then right. Repeat this movement several times, noticing again as you pass through the center point. Return to the center. When you have found your center, you will feel poised and relaxed, at one with gravity, and that you are sitting more effortlessly than usual.

The Standing Posture

We spend much of the day standing, but rarely pay much attention to it unless we're having a physical problem that's causing discomfort. The following exercise shows you how to pay attention to standing as an activity in itself. You can use standing as a meditation position, like sitting, when you are formally engaging in meditative practice. You can also attend to standing wherever you are. You may be surprised that you become more comfortable and relaxed in your everyday life as you become more aware of how you stand.

Exercise 4.2   Awareness of Standing

Stand upright with your feet approximately shoulder-width apart and eyes either closed or open. If you feel a little dizzy when you close your eyes, keep them open. Pay attention to how your feet relate to the floor surface. Do they seem to be pressing down on the floor, or does the floor seem to be pressing up on your feet? Do your feet feel hard, soft, warm, or cool? Is your whole foot making contact, or is the most weight on your heels or forward on your toes? There are many possibilities. Now focus attention on your legs in the same way. Do your legs feel sturdy or weak, loose or tight, as they support your weight? Move your attention up to your midsection, chest, and back. Notice your breathing while you are standing, and notice how your chest and back move as you breathe. Now, pay attention to your neck and head. Is your neck tight? If so, notice where you feel the tension. Are you standing with your head thrust forward, or is it held upright, centered, and in balance? Now let your attention roam throughout your body as you stand. Don't change anything unless it occurs naturally. Do not label the experience with words. Instead simply stand attentively, just feeling the sensations of standing. After a few minutes move on to the next exercise.

Exercise 4.3   Find Your Standing Posture

Stand with your legs shoulder-width apart at a comfortable distance, with your feet flat on the ground, hands at your sides, head upright, and eyes looking ahead—at ease. Now, rock gently back and forth, forward and back on the balls of your feet, and then on your heels— back and forth, forward and back. Concentrate on the sensations. With each swaying motion, there is a point in the middle where your muscles are less tense and your body is most at ease. Slowly reduce the sway so that you arrive at this balance point, at ease, aligned, and still.

Next, move the same way from side to side, gently rocking slowly so that your weight shifts first to one foot and then to the other. Gradually reduce the motion until you find a point in the center where your muscles are the most relaxed, with your weight evenly distributed on both feet. This is the exact balance point where your body is best aligned with gravity. Repeat this exercise several times to ensure that you have found the best center point. If possible, let go of any unnecessary tensions. Enjoy the solidity of this pose for a few moments.

The Lying-Down Posture

We sleep lying down, so many people find that it's easier to relax and be calm while they are lying down. Life is always about relationship. When you're lying down, your body is in relationship with the supporting surface. We rarely think of lying down as more than the act itself, but it can become a useful position for meditation. Often, meditating while lying down feels easier because of the support given by the floor. You can learn about yourself through this relationship with the floor or couch that you lie on.

Even though you are lying down, like when you sleep, meditation is different from sleep. If you find yourself getting drowsy when lying down, begin with a sitting or standing position. Once you are more adept at meditation, you will find that using these positions makes you feel more alert and less tired. The position you choose should be the one that's most comfortable for you.

Exercise 4.4   Find Your Lying-Down Posture on Your Back

Begin by attending to how you move into the prone position. Move smoothly and slowly into position as you lie down on your back on the floor, with legs and arms extended, palms facing down. Let your body relax as you keep your attention focused on the movement. Once you are in position, let your feet move apart slightly. Close your eyes and breathe comfortably. Scan your body with your attention, and let go of any unnecessary tension. You may notice extra tension in the muscles of your face, stomach, neck, shoulders, or back. If so, let it go. Relax more deeply with each passing moment. Rest in this position for a few minutes.

If you feel tightness in your lower back, raise your knees while leaving your feet flat on the floor. You may want to put a pillow under your knees and let your legs extend comfortably. This tends to let the lower back flatten, allowing it to relax very deeply. As you feel your back muscles let go, you may be able to extend your legs flat. If not, use the modified position to allow yourself to relax when needed. When you feel ready, come out of the position, continuing to be aware through the entire process as you bring yourself to standing once again.

Exercise 4.5   Find Your Lying-Down Posture on Your Front

A second lying-down position is to rest facedown on the floor. Let your legs stretch apart at a comfortable distance, with your heels facing in and toes pointing out. Bend your arms to make a resting place for your forehead, and allow yourself to totally relax. Gently breathe in and out as you let go of any unnecessary tensions.

Honing Your Meditation Tools

Sometimes people think that meditating is something mysterious and obscure. But in reality, it draws on down-to-earth, everyday skills that you already have but may not be using. Attention, imagination, body awareness, and the mind-body link are your tools for meditation. You use them whenever you meditate. You may not realize that you can hone these meditation tools, much like how a chef sharpens knives before using them for cutting. Practice these exercises several times, and you will notice your tools becoming more accessible over time. Begin with just a few minutes for each of the exercises in this section, and increase the time as you feel able to do so.

Exercise 4.6 Attention and Imagination

Pick something to look at: a painting you like, a beautiful plant, or even a piece of technology you like to use. Just make sure it's something that you find interesting to look at. Place it in clear view and sit down. Look carefully at this object for a minute or so. Focus all your attention on it. Notice the colors, shape, texture, or anything else that you see. Don't look at anything else. If your mind wanders, gently bring it back to viewing the object. When you feel that you have a clear sense of this object, close your eyes and try to picture it as best you can. Some people will see a vivid image, and others will just have a vague memory of it. Whatever you see, keep your attention focused on the image of the object. Give yourself a minute or two to conjure up the image. If you find that you have missed some of the details, open your eyes and look again. Then, close your eyes and imagine the object once more. You may want to open and close your eyes several times until you feel that you have captured a somewhat accurate sense of the object. Try the exercise with different objects.

Exercise 4.7 Body Awareness

Sometimes we ask our clients to turn their attention to the body, to notice any sensations they might be feeling. Some people can do this easily, but others find it difficult to do. Part of being able to notice body experiences involves taking a moment to deliberately pay attention to subtle cues.

Sit quietly for a moment and turn your attention to your body sensations. Everyone has felt a tight muscle from time to time. Can you turn your attention to your muscles and notice whether some muscles might be tight while others are relaxed? You have also probably noticed your body temperature when you have walked outdoors on a very cold or hot day. Can you notice the temperature of your hands or your face now as you are sitting indoors? Allow your attention to wander around through your body and notice any other body sensations, such as growling in your stomach if you are feeling hungry, or the movement of your chest up and down as you breathe. Take a few minutes to notice whatever you are experiencing now in your body as you sit quietly.

Exercise 4.8   The Ideomotor Mind-Body Link

Your tools of attention and body are linked together automatically through a natural mechanism known as the *ideomotor link*. When you think about something, it tends to be expressed in your body. Here is a way to experience this direct mind-body link.

Sit quietly, close your eyes, and imagine that you are sucking on a *very* tart lemon. As you vividly imagine the lemon resting on your tongue, does your mouth automatically begin to water a bit? The watering in your mouth occurs because of the ideomotor link. Your thought immediately produced a response in your body.

Now sit quietly and imagine a time when you felt completely relaxed and comfortable. Perhaps you were on vacation or enjoying time with loved ones at home. Vividly picture yourself enjoying this experience. Recall any key details, such as how things looked around you, what you did, and how you felt. If you are able to recall this experience vividly, you will notice that your body begins to relax automatically. You don't have to change anything in your body to make it happen. You simply allow your body to respond naturally to the memory of being completely relaxed. This is the ideomotor link in action.

You will use all of these tools to help you when you meditate. As you familiarize yourself with how you pay attention, as you vividly imagine, as you notice your body experiencing, and as you allow your mind-body link to develop, you are beginning to walk the path to your Tao. You become aware of your inner nature, not as an abstraction but through concrete experiencing. And this inner nature will become an additional resource for you in overcoming the symptoms of your bipolar disorder.

Conclusion

This chapter has provided a guide for beginning to meditate. Find your meditation space, make some time, and experiment with each of the positions to sense which ones seem most comfortable to you. We will advise when to use a particular posture in the coming chapters, but please feel free to experiment with more than one if you would like. Whatever position you choose to take during meditation, you will find that paying close attention to your posture will help you to discover a sense of balance in your body. Becoming aware of your posture, whether or not it is balanced, is a step on the path to emotional balance in general.

You have begun using your tools of meditation: attention, imagination, body, and their links. As you become more skilled in meditation, you will develop an inner sense of what feels natural for you. We encourage you to listen to the subtle cues you receive from your own inner experiencing.

Meditation is a natural ability that begins small. You don't need fancy equipment or special talents. Just begin where you are, with just a few minutes at a time. Your skills will build. Be patient with yourself as you practice. In time, you will not only feel more at ease with meditation, but also begin to notice a gradual reduction in your mood swings. Many people around the world and through the ages have shared in the tradition of meditation, and you can too! Have confidence in your ability to enjoy the experience and gain positive benefits for more balance in your life.

Chapter 5

Focus on Breathing: The Gateway to Moods

Breathing is a perfect expression of the body's wisdom. The Tao of breathing is present from birth, when you take your first breath, and remains a constant throughout your life. You know how to breathe, and rarely think about it unless it's a problem. Breathing has a great deal to do with many aspects of your life. It is linked to your energy, known as chi, as we discussed in chapter 1. The word "chi" corresponds to conceptions found in the Greek word *pneuma* and the Sanskrit word *prana*, meaning breath, respiration, wind, and especially vitality. Breathing is connected to energy, and as we described in earlier chapters, your energy corresponds to your mood. Breathing is also directly linked to emotion. When you have a strong feeling, your breathing usually changes, becoming rapid. And when you are feeling relaxed, breathing slows. Because of the close interaction among breathing, energy, and emotions, altering your breathing affects your moods.

Breathing meditations lead to skills in noticing, guiding, and transforming the flow of chi through the body, and by doing so, you regulate your moods. By turning your attention to your breathing, you can know what you are feeling from the inside. You can ease a mood or moderate a strong emotion. Meditating on your breathing helps you bring about a comfortable balance.

The ability to maintain your attention on breathing teaches a broader skill of directing focus to any object of your choice. Focusing is one of the three fundamental meditative methods you will learn in this book. This chapter includes instructions for how to narrow your focus and keep it steady. You will use this valuable skill in part 3 to overcome much of the discomfort you may be suffering. This chapter also incorporates some of the best classic breathing meditations through the ages to help you get in touch with your breathing patterns. We include some simple ways to calm and relax the breath, and show you how to use breathing methods even in the midst of strong emotion to help moderate your moods. The final meditations in this chapter help you become centered in each breath. Profound calm develops, putting you in tune with your deeper nature, at one with the Tao, leading to improved health and balanced vitality.

The Breath of Life Is Vital to Your Moods

Your body knows how to breathe, and it takes care of breathing automatically. This process is directed from the respiratory centers in the brain stem. But breathing is unique because, unlike other involuntary processes, such as digestion, breathing can also be voluntary, directed from the thinking brain in your cortex. Meditation works with the voluntary control of breathing.

Breathing rate changes automatically when you are having a strong emotion or feeling stressed. However, when you practice focusing your attention on breathing, you produce a shift in your autonomic nervous system, which makes your breathing calmer and strong emotions more moderate. Recent research is finding that there is breathing neuroplasticity. People can develop breathing problems from anxiety or weight gain, two issues that you may be dealing with. Research shows that you can enhance breathing plasticity in positive ways through exercise (Feldman, Mitchell, and Nattie 2003). Meditation offers a method of breath control that can also enhance positive respiratory plasticity.

The breathing meditations taught in this chapter produce the dual simultaneous effects of calmness and alertness (review chapter 3 for more information). Your sympathetic nervous system is deactivated while the parasympathetic nervous system is activated, which accounts for the calming effect. At the same time, by keeping your attention focused, you become more alert and energized (Jerath et al. 2006). Being calm while alert tends to regulate your moods.

Experiment with all of the meditations presented in this chapter. People vary in what they need, so we suggest doing them all in the sequence presented. One method may feel more natural and easier to you than another. If you find that one of these meditations seems easier to do, repeat that one often. As you become skilled in doing it, you build a bridge to the other breathing methods. Eventually, we encourage you to practice all of these breathing meditations, as feels appropriate.

Classic Breathing Meditations

Begin the process when you are feeling relatively comfortable. Consider that you are building a skill now. Then, when you are upset or uncomfortable, you will be able to easily slip into meditation to lessen your discomforts and ease your mood.

Exercise 5.1 Begin by Counting the Breaths

Start with this meditation on breathing. It is easy to do and helps you begin. Practice it several times until you can keep your attention focused on breathing for several minutes.

Sit comfortably, in a way that allows your breathing passages to be free. So, don't slouch down, but also don't hold yourself rigidly upright either. Just sit up relatively straight and comfortably. Breathe through your nose as you normally do when sitting quietly. Inwardly count each complete breath, in and out. Begin with one and count each breath up to ten. Breathe normally, without trying to change anything. When you get to ten, start over with your counting and go up to ten again. Remember not to breathe harder or faster; just breathe normally and count every breath. If your thoughts wander away from counting, gently bring yourself back to counting as soon as you notice. Keep counting for several minutes. When you are finished, open your eyes, and stand up and stretch.

Exercise 5.2   Follow the Breath

For this exercise, sit cross-legged on a pillow, sit on a chair, or lie down on the floor on your back. Most important is to allow your breathing passages to be relatively relaxed. Breathe through your nose, not your mouth.

Close your eyes and turn your attention to your breathing. Notice the air as it comes in through your nose, and then flows down into your lungs and out again. Pay close attention to how your chest, diaphragm, stomach, and back move as you breathe. Don't interfere with the natural pattern of breathing. Just relax and breathe normally as you keep your attention focused on the process of breathing. If your attention wanders, gently bring it back to focus on breathing.

For those who find this exercise difficult to do, return to the previous exercise. All of these meditations improve with practice.

Exercise 5.3   The Complete Breath

Drawn from yoga pranayama practice, the complete breath frees your breathing, without forcing it. Breathing becomes full naturally, for maximum benefit from a minimum expenditure of energy.

Stand comfortably, but as straight as possible without straining. Turn your attention to your breathing. Breathe in steadily through your nose. Allow the air to fill the upper section of your lungs by letting your diaphragm contract and push the air down into the middle part of your lungs, pushing out the lower ribs and chest. Draw the air all the way down to fill the lower part of your abdomen, allowing it to expand. Do so in one smooth inhalation, permitting your chest cavity to expand in all directions. Retain the breath for a few seconds. Then exhale very slowly, beginning from the abdomen. Draw your abdomen in gently, lifting it slightly as the air leaves your lungs. Keep your attention focused on your body as the air flows all the way out. Repeat the complete breath, in and out, three times. Then stand for several minutes, breathing gently and sensing your body. You may find that you feel refreshed and vitalized.

Another way to experience the complete breath more fully is by placing your hands lightly over your abdomen. You should feel an in-and-out movement in your abdomen as the air enters and leaves. You don't need to take deep breaths. Simply keep your breathing as natural as possible, and stay relaxed throughout.

Exercise 5.4   Rhythmic Breathing

Rhythmic breathing helps you integrate two rhythms of your body: your pulse and your breathing.

Feel your heart rate by placing your fingers on your wrist to take your pulse. Count six beats, one to six, and then repeat until the rhythm becomes fixed in your mind. Next, turn your attention to your breathing. Sit in a comfortable posture, with your back straight, shoulders open, and hands resting gently on your lap. Keep your rib cage and chest relaxed and flexible.

Gently inhale a complete breath (from the previous exercise), counting six beats paced to your pulse. Hold your breath for three counts, and then exhale slowly through your nose, counting six pulse beats. Repeat, breathing gently in this way.

Calming Breathing

The next set of meditations will teach you how to calm your breathing.

The first meditation in this section teaches how to permit and let be. Often we try too hard. You might think that you have to *make* yourself calm your breathing. But, one of the greatest lessons of Taoism is to learn how to allow change to happen naturally, to do without ado, as the Tao Te Ching teaches. Your body knows how to breathe naturally. This meditation returns you to instinctive, relaxed breathing.

The second meditation shows you how to reclaim the early, natural wisdom of a child to be spontaneously at ease. You probably can recall times when you were very young, so this ability is built into your memories, just waiting to be accessed to help you now. Practice these two exercises in sequence for several minutes each. Increase the time to fifteen minutes each, as you are able to do so.

Exercise 5.5   Allow Breathing

Sit or lie down in a comfortable position. Simply notice what you experience. Observe your breathing. Is it easy? Labored? Slow? Quick? Notice without changing anything. In this approach, you don't try to change your breathing; rather, you allow the change to take place naturally as you simply observe. Can you allow your whole rib cage to take part in your breathing? Can you permit your abdomen to relax and move with your breathing? Can you feel your lower back and waist move? Can you feel your shoulders move? Breathe just as you do, without interfering or holding the breath back, while not trying to breathe deeper or shallower. Wait and allow your body to respond naturally and automatically. Eventually your breath will find its way to a natural, comfortable rhythm.

Exercise 5.6   Breathe Like a Child

In the Tao Te Ching is written, "In concentrating your breath and making it soft, can you make it like that of a child?" (Lao-tzu 1989, 62). You can use the image of a peacefully sleeping child to help you calm your breathing.

You have probably watched a young child sleeping. The breathing is soft, smooth, and easy. With that image in mind, find a comfortable position. Let your breathing be soft and calm. Place your hands on your rib cage to feel the movement in and out, rising and falling. Let each breath be light and gentle, like that of a child. Let go of any unnecessary tension. If you would like, do the complete breath exercise, keeping each breath supple, soft, and natural. Breathe softly for several minutes, calming and centering yourself.

Moderating Moods through Breathing

Tears may well up as you heave a sigh of sadness. You may barely dare to breathe as your heart pounds with fear. You may gasp for breath as your face burns red and your anger surges. Strong emotions bring distinctive changes in breathing. And yet, deep within the sea of emotions, you can find your Tao. Meditation helps you navigate through the choppy waters. By using the rhythms of your breathing as your compass and remaining in tune with the Tao, you discover calm currents in the ocean.

So, attention to breathing can help you regulate your emotions. The first exercise in this section attunes you to your feelings through the breath. The next exercise teaches you how to use breathing to relieve discomfort from your moods, a valuable skill that you can turn to when you are feeling uncomfortable emotions.

You can begin by practicing the first exercise alone, but as soon as you feel able to sustain your practice for five or ten minutes, try doing the two exercises in sequence, one after the other.

Exercise 5.7   Become Aware of Your Emotions

Use this exercise when you are having different emotions to compare and contrast. Paying attention to breathing while in the midst of many different feelings will teach you about yourself and your reactions, adding clarity to your emotions. You may find that your uncomfortable feelings begin to lessen somewhat or even dissolve completely.

Sit down and take a moment to turn your attention to breathing when you are feeling extremely happy, sad, angry, stressed, tired, or any emotion that you typically feel. Notice the rhythm of your breath. Is it fast or slow? What is its quality: pushed, labored, shallow, or perhaps deep? Pay attention to surrounding muscles in your rib cage, neck, face, and back. Do you perceive patterns of tension? Sit quietly and feel any other sensations that accompany your breathing when you have this feeling, such as hot or cold, tingling or numbness. Also, note what thoughts you are having. If you would like to alter the

79

feeling, sit a little longer and try some of the previous exercises for permitting, relaxing, or controlling the breath. You may feel the intensity of the emotion begin to subside slightly.

Later, repeat this exercise when you are having another feeling. Compare and contrast the quality of breathing during different emotions. Getting to know what your breathing is like when you feel different emotions and moods is helpful for bringing about change.

Exercise 5.8 Regulate Your Emotions Naturally through Breath

The Taoist conceives of the human body as being in harmony with the cosmos: the internal corresponds with the external, the mind with the body. Each of us is a microcosm of the great macrocosm, comprising a mixture of yin and yang, heaven and earth. Moving meditations can help you feel the links between mind and body, breathing and energy. Coordinating body movements with breathing brings more awareness while also fostering the free flow of energy to remove blockages, relieve anxiety, and regulate overly strong moods. Movements are done slowly, without tension, to promote free circulation of chi.

Stand with your feet shoulder-width apart and facing forward. Take a few relaxed, natural breaths. Next, extend your arms out straight in front of you, at shoulder height and parallel to the floor as you exhale. Then, as you breathe in, extend your arms out to each side, with your hands open and fingers apart, relaxing your arms a bit and letting your elbows sink slightly. Allow your rib cage to expand with your inhalation. Hold for a count of three, and then bring your arms back to the front as you exhale. Repeat with slow, even movements and soft, easy breaths for several minutes. As you do these movements, visualize the air moving out from your lungs to the very tips of your fingers and down through your legs to your toes. Let breathing motions flow in coordination with your whole body, freely and comfortably.

Finally, let your arms drop down to your sides again, and then breathe naturally and comfortably, aware of each breath in and out. As you practice these gentle movements and coordinate them with your breathing, you are likely to experience a mild shift in your mood. People often feel revitalized, a little more relaxed, and generally more aware of themselves in the present moment. You may even feel a slight tingling and vitality all over. When you feel ready to stop moving, stand quietly for a moment, breathing as you pay attention.

Conclusion

Breathing is vital to the health of your body and brain. You are always breathing, and when you feel any emotion, your breathing alters somewhat. Thus, an excellent place to begin your journey is to become more aware of your breathing and then be able to start moderating your mood through the breath. Turn your attention to your breathing throughout your day, and allow it to become steady and calm. The more often you practice, the stronger the effects. In addition, you may find the breathing exercises to be accessible and enjoyable. Working with the breath can bring benefits that include moments of comfort and well-being.

Chapter 6

Open Focus: Developing Mindful Awareness

Real change begins with awareness, and you can enhance awareness with meditation. Mindfulness is a form of self-awareness with a different way of seeing things. As you become more mindful, you become conscious of your moods as they are happening. You can follow subtle shifts just as a change begins to happen, attuning to your personal Tao and the Tao of your mood swings. With this knowledge, you open the option for choosing something different. In addition, mindfulness brings more moderation of your emotions, so as you practice meditation, your mood swings tend to become less severe.

The exercises in this chapter break mindfulness down into manageable parts. We begin with mindfulness of body and then feelings, followed by thoughts. The final mindfulness exercise develops an overall mindful presence, grounded in each moment. By opening the focus of your attention you will enrich the quality of your experience and discover more enjoyment.

You can do the mindfulness series in this chapter in two ways. One way is to do each meditation in sequence, spending between two and five minutes on each one, going through the entire series. As an alternative, spend more time on one of the mindfulness exercises. Practice it at different times of the day and in different settings.

Once you are skilled with mindfulness meditations, you will be able to take a mindful glance at any time, wherever you are and whatever you are doing. Later chapters will show you how to use your mindfulness skills to moderate your moods.

What Is Mindfulness?

Mindfulness is an experience that brings your attention to the present moment. What you attend to is always changing, resulting in an open focus of your attention. Instead of drawing conclusions about what you are experiencing, you just notice the experience itself. So, for example, if you hear a noise, you don't try to figure out what caused the noise; you simply listen to the sound. You hear the tones, the volume, and the silence after the noise stops. You recognize how each moment is new, and let your attention follow the ever-changing flow as it unfolds.

Mindfulness is an approach to life, a way of orienting yourself with alert awareness and complete presence. The word "mindfulness" implies its meaning: mind-*full*-ness, a method that fills the mind completely with each experience. It's not just a matter of what you do, but rather how you apply your attention to it. Life without mindfulness is foggy and vague, driven by blind impulse and external pressures. But a life with awareness opens the potential to engage fully in your life and to do so with wisdom.

Research on mindfulness shows that by activating your attention in this way, you stimulate neuroplasticity in your brain. Sara Lazar and her research group have been actively exploring the effects of mindfulness on neuroplasticity (review chapter 3). Lazar's group recently found that after an eight-week course in mindfulness, participants showed increases in regional gray-matter density in the hippocampus, cingulate gyrus, and temporal-parietal junction (Hölzel et al. 2011). These brain areas tend to be smaller in people with bipolar disorder. Increasing the gray matter in these areas is known to be helpful for managing your moods. So, if you engage in the regular practice of mindfulness, you are likely to improve the functioning in key areas that will help your bipolar symptoms.

Mindfulness has also been found to reduce stress (Grossman et al. 2004), and stress often triggers a bipolar episode. Through regular mindfulness practice, you will feel less stressed. You will have a better sense of what you need to do to stabilize your moods, and even recognize the signs that may allow you to prevent an episode from getting started.

Mindfulness begins with you in your own experience, here and now. Work with the exercises to develop your skills. Use your body, feelings, thoughts, and moment-by-moment presence. In time, your awareness will spread into every moment, like a light that illuminates the darkness.

Taking a Nonjudgmental Attitude

Mindfulness gives you the opportunity to get to know more about yourself. This knowledge can be helpful at times, but occasionally you may not like what you observe. As a result, you might be tempted to pass judgment on yourself. But judging yourself will not help you to moderate your moodiness. In fact, it may interfere.

Mindful awareness is nonjudgmental. What this means is that you should not jump to conclusions or use the new information you gain from being mindful to form biased opinions. Like a scientist who is gathering data, wait until you have more of the facts. Trust the process and cultivate an open mind. The Tao is found in the undifferentiated flow of experience. So, returning to just what you feel and think in the present moment will center you in your deeper nature. Suspending opinions and judgments *about* your experience takes you a step toward the Tao. So let your judgmental thoughts go when you do mindfulness meditation, and you will find yourself in tune with the Tao.

As you first practice mindfulness, you might feel tempted to judge yourself negatively if you notice something about yourself that you don't like. Instead of saying how bad you are or how much you dislike something about yourself, simply take note that you don't like it, but don't criticize yourself. There's an important difference between observing something that may need changing and moralizing against it. You may eventually decide that what you have observed is a quality you would like to change but that doing so is premature at this point. Instead, whenever you can, simply observe. Observe without making judgmental pronouncements: just follow what you are experiencing, moment by moment. The mysteries of your inner mind will open up as you become alert, centered, and aware.

Exercise 6.1 Self-Acceptance

You can begin learning mindfulness by practicing a nonjudgmental attitude. Start now by noticing some details about your appearance. You probably have opinions about how you look: you might like your hair but dislike your height and so on. In this exercise, we invite you to set aside all these judgments, both good and bad. Your mood swings may be influenced by these likes and dislikes, so learning how to accept yourself fully, as you are, can have a moderating influence on your moods.

Observe yourself from head to toe and recognize all your different parts. You may look in a mirror or use another way to observe. Describe each part to yourself. Notice, for example, your hair—its color, texture, style—your eyes, and so on. But stay factual. For example, observe that your eyes are brown, a certain distance apart, with long lashes or thick eyebrows. But don't add an evaluation, such as "unattractive" or "too close together." Being nonjudgmental can help you to accept yourself, even if you believe that you have serious deficiencies. Embrace what you are and what you feel, without belittling yourself.

Mindful of Body

Now that you have started to work on being nonjudgmental, you are ready to begin mindfulness meditations about the body, emotions, and thoughts. Make your observations without judging what you notice as good or bad. Just notice. As you do so, you open the way to get in tune with the Tao of your experiencing, allowing it to flow moment by moment, just as it is.

Exercise 6.2   Open Attention to Body Experiences

Sit comfortably and turn your attention to your body. Begin by paying attention to your skin. Does it feel cool or warm, dry or damp? Do you have any sensations such as tingling, itching, or pain in a particular body area? You may not have noticed any sensations. Notice mindfully without judging the sensation as good or bad; just notice it now. Move inward to your muscles. Scan through your body and pay attention to different muscle groups, beginning with your facial muscles and moving down through your body. Notice the sensations you feel there, perhaps a tight feeling or heaviness.

Notice what you experience, but don't try to change anything. Just be aware. Then, moving further inward, turn to your breathing as you did in the exercises in chapter 5. Notice as the air comes in through your nose, goes down into your lungs, and then travels out again. Does the air feel warm or cool? Is your breathing soft or forced? Follow each breath in and out. Although breathing may seem like an unchanging process, recognize that each breath is new. Now turn your attention to your pulse. Although it may be difficult to sense at first, be patient, and you might begin to feel the sensation. If not, place your fingers on your pulse at the inside of your wrist. Finally, allow your attention to move all around your body, and notice any sensations that occur. Sit quietly for several minutes with your attention focused on sensations.

Mindful of Feelings

Emotions are an important component of living, so mindfulness must include attention to feelings. Mindfulness gives you a strategy for dealing with emotions in a way that will overcome suffering from uncomfortable feelings and maximize fulfillment from positive ones.

Feelings can be categorized as pleasant, unpleasant, or neutral. People tend to cling to pleasant feelings and reject unpleasant ones. But this clinging and rejecting sets in motion a secondary set of reactions that interferes with awareness and causes suffering. Of course, you want to be happy and to have things that bring you pleasure, but the things of life that people enjoy inevitably change. The new car you purchase today becomes the old, used car you try to sell tomorrow. Being too attached to your pleasures will bring suffering when they end. Impermanence is good news for suffering, because even the worst pain will pass, so being too worried about it will only make it worse. Letting go of the secondary reaction helps you to be more aware of the feelings themselves, which leads to more comfortable, aware, and enlightened reactions.

Exercise 6.3   Identify Feelings

Mindfulness of feelings begins when you can identify the emotion you are having. To start the process, sit down for a moment and close your eyes. Turn your attention inward. Try to put a name to your emotion or mood. Then match the description with what you feel. If it's not quite right, modify your description until you feel satisfied.

Be benevolent with yourself, like a kindergarten teacher who watches over the students as they play on the playground. When two children begin fighting, the teacher doesn't become angry with them but, instead, tries to calmly attend to their needs. Benevolently observe all your different feelings, even the ones you don't like. By eliminating the secondary aversion reaction to a negative feeling, you will significantly lessen your suffering.

Exercise 6.4   Stay with Feelings

Now that you have identified your feeling, allow yourself to sit quietly, just feeling your emotion. Notice the sensations and experience just as it is. Don't label it or judge it; simply stay with the feeling. Notice how it changes a bit with each passing moment. Perhaps your breathing slows or a sensation in your stomach appears or diminishes. Stay with the experience for several minutes, and extend the time as you are able to do so. Try this exercise at different times, when you are feeling different emotions.

Mindful of Thoughts

Mindfulness of thoughts involves observing your mental activity itself. Mental processes take on many different forms, filling our minds with one thought after another. At times, we think with clarity, while at other times, our thoughts are confused. Sometimes the mind is filled with emotion, and other times it's completely unemotional. But if you step back and look at the broader picture, you notice that all of these different states of mind are actually composed of mental processes. For example, if you look at a flower, the flower you see is really a product of your cognitive activity, constructed by your mind. In fact, everything you perceive is partly mentally constructed. Through mindful awareness, you can step outside your usual mental constructs.

Exercise 6.5   Become Aware of Thoughts

Sit quietly and close your eyes. Follow the flow of your thought. Notice what you are thinking about as you think it. So, if you are thinking about what you have to do later today, notice *that* you are thinking now about what you have to do later. You might find it helpful to say to yourself, *Now I am thinking this; now I am thinking that.*

Be like someone who is sitting on the bank of a river watching leaves and twigs flow downstream. Don't jump into the river. Stay onshore, observing. So, don't let yourself get carried away by a stream of thought. Just keep observing each thought in each moment. If you find yourself drifting downstream with a thought, climb back onshore and resume your observing as soon as you notice this happening.

Now observe beyond the content of thinking to thought itself. Notice your stream of thinking as it flows. Do you have many thoughts all at once? Or are your thoughts slow? Do you tend to think about a certain thing or person? Or are your thoughts scattered, jumping from topic to topic? Don't judge a thought as good or bad; just notice the different qualities of your thinking. This kind of observing takes practice, so be patient. Try it for short periods at first, even as little as one minute, and extend duration as you are able.

Exercise 6.6 Recognize Helpful and Harmful Thoughts about Bipolar Disorder

Some of your thoughts are helpful and realistic, while others are unrealistic and biased. Specifically, you may have a set of thoughts about your bipolar disorder that makes your symptoms more difficult to handle and that may even make them worse. For example, you may become discouraged from negative experiences and believe that you can't really improve your condition. If so, you may miss opportunities to make things better. Your thoughts can also help you at times. When you believe that you *can* do something to help your bipolar symptoms, you will be open to making efforts to help yourself. In addition, you will feel encouraged and hopeful, sentiments that tend to help you to feel better and endure difficulties well.

List your beliefs about your bipolar disorder. Note whether, deep down, you hold a belief that you will never change. Objectively describe exactly what this belief is and why you think it. For example, one typical belief is that bipolar disorder is a disease that is genetically determined and can't be changed. Clarify just what your thoughts are about bipolar disorder and then move on to the next exercise.

Exercise 6.7 Go to the Roots of Beliefs

Mindful meditation on where some of your ideas about bipolar disorder came from can help you to weed out those thoughts and beliefs that are preventing you from changing. If you found in the previous exercise that you believe there is little you can do, trace this belief back to its roots. Where does it come from? Did you learn it from someone else? Or maybe you read some stories of people who were unable to control their symptoms, and then you became convinced that you, too, would be helpless to change. Or perhaps it comes from your own self-doubt, that even if others can do it, you can't. Trace your belief to its origins, make note of this, and question whether keeping this belief is in your best interest. Chapter 9 will help you challenge beliefs that may be holding you back.

You can do more than just be mindful of your beliefs. You can also cultivate encouraging beliefs about your bipolar disorder, and discourage unrealistic and destructive ones. Look for evidence, such as what is presented in this book, of the many things you can do to improve your condition. Just as a farmer nourishes plants with the proper soil, sunlight, and water, so should you nourish your thoughts with realistic hopes, encouragement, and openness to possibilities.

Mindful in the Moment

Fritz Perls (1969), founder of gestalt therapy, said that awareness is curative. What he meant was that by our simply being mindfully aware, things change by themselves. You may be pleasantly surprised to discover how these wise words ring true. By simply practicing mindfulness, without any goal in mind, your discomforts will ease. Part 3 will more extensively apply this and other forms of meditation to assist you with overcoming your problems and finding a healthier and more comfortable balance.

Exercise 6.8   Be Mindful Now

Now that you have experimented with various ways of being mindful, you can bring them all together in the present moment. Turn your attention to your body to increase your body awareness. Be mindful of your emotions by observing what you are feeling. Notice your mental activity. What are you thinking or perceiving? Observe all of these qualities quickly, like scanning a horizon to take in everything all at once. You will notice that a shift occurs as you become more centered in the here and now. Stay aware as new experiences unfold. Keep noticing whatever you sense, feel, or think for several minutes. Let your attention flow to each new experience that you are having now. If your attention drifts, bring it back to your process of mindful observing as soon as you notice. Don't try to change how you are; just let yourself be fully present.

Conclusion

Practice mindfulness meditation often and you will find that your skill improves over time. Notice how your experience transforms. Stay with each new moment. Whenever you can, at various points during the day, turn your attention to your experience. Get in touch mindfully as often as you can. In time, mindfulness will feel natural. You may begin to have periods when you feel in balance with yourself and your surroundings, accepting the flow of life as it comes and acting in harmony with what you need.

Chapter 7

No Focus: Clearing Your Mind

There once was a person who suffered from severe shifts in moods. He (or maybe she; it was so long ago that the records are lost) had been seeking treatment for many years. He had built up many ideas about his problems and was quite convinced that he was unlucky in life. Although he hadn't given up on trying to help himself, he felt discouraged about ever getting better. He heard about a great meditation master and thought that maybe meditation could help him. So he decided to seek out this master to learn meditation. When he arrived, a servant came to the door. The visitor said, "I have bipolar disorder and was hoping the master could help me with meditation. I know a lot about my problems. I have tried all kinds of treatments, but I'm still suffering. I heard about the master's methods. Please ask him if he will accept me as his student." The servant welcomed him in and said, "Please wait." The servant returned in a few minutes and said, "I relayed your message to the master, and he asked if you would like to join him for tea." The student was pleased, and thanked the servant as he followed him into the office.

The master smiled and motioned for the student to sit down with him on a straw mat. As the master began preparing the tea, the student thought he should tell the master about himself. He said, "I know a lot about my problem. I know it affects the brain. I've heard that mania could be a defense against depression, and I believe that genetics is part of the problem. I think it's a lifelong problem, and I probably can't do much about it. But I tried doing cognitive therapy, I've done group therapy, and I—"

The master continued preparing the tea without saying a word while the student kept up a running stream of conversation. "I know a lot about meditation. I believe in direct perception, but I'm not too clear on emptiness. I wonder if emptiness is something or nothing." While the master placed the tea leaves in the pot, the student watched, saying, "I know a lot about tea. There's oolong tea and green tea. You know, green tea is really good for you, and then, of course, herbal teas are healthy too. I like peppermint tea, although it doesn't have caffeine, and I really like caffeine!"

The master silently handed him a cup. The student scrutinized the cup and said, "What a beautiful cup! I know a lot about cups! There are cups from China that are very delicate. Korean cups are often unsigned, because they like the idea of an anonymous artist. My favorite kind of cups are the older ones."

The master silently began pouring. The student continued talking: "I know a lot about pouring! Did you know that in England they pour tea from two pots, one with tea and the other with hot water? And you have a nice way of pouring."

As the student chattered on and on, the master kept pouring and pouring. The cup filled higher and higher, until the tea began spilling out onto the mat.

Startled, the student said, "Master, Master! My cup is overflowing!"

The master smiled and said simply, "As is your mind. First empty your cup, and then it can be filled!"

This classic meditation story illustrates an important point. Your mind is filled with a continual stream of thoughts. When you are manic, your thoughts move quickly with ever-flowing ideas. And when you are depressed, although you may think more slowly, you continually ruminate critically about yourself and others. Typically, the thinking you do in either mood may interfere with meeting new possibilities openly.

Clearing your mind has a profound effect. It is especially helpful when you are trying to make a change. So, we invite you to empty your cup. The meditations in this chapter teach you the third form of meditation used in this book, no-focus meditations to clear your mind. You learn to let go of those thoughts and impulses that may be getting in your way. In addition, this type of meditation helps you to create a fertile void, the empty moment, where new potentials can emerge more easily and naturally. You find your balance point in the empty moment. So, by clearing away the stream of thoughts that interrupt the empty moment, you pave the way for change.

Meditation for clearing the mind has been found to bring about neuroplasticity in the brain that is helpful to bipolar disorder. A recent study showed increase in gray matter in the cingulate gyrus, anterior insula, and hippocampus when people practiced a Zen meditation for clearing the mind (Grant et al. 2010). Increasing the size of these brain areas will help you to regulate your emotions better, increase your awareness of inner experiencing, and improve your memory.

Letting Go to Clear Consciousness

Experiment with the following exercises to develop the ability to clear your mind. Be patient; these exercises do respond to practice. And keep in mind that stable, consistent practice is healthy. But focus on the experience of the exercise, not on the exercise just as a means to an end. Without a goal in mind, simply enjoy each experience for itself and let your abilities develop naturally.

The series of five exercises presented here will lead you step by step into clearing your mind. We also offer you several alternative methods. Some ways of emptying your mind might feel more natural to you than others. Try all the exercises once. Then repeat them, and work longer with the ones that seem easiest for you to do. As your skills develop, you will be able to spend more time on the ones that seem harder. Begin with one minute for each exercise, but work up to at least five minutes as soon as you are able to do so. Do the exercises at different times of day. You may discover that some times are better than others. You will continue to develop your skills by using variations of these meditations in part 3. You are beginning a process here, one that ripens over time.

To Try or Not to Try

You might think that clearing the mind means trying to stop all your thoughts, but it's not what you might expect. You don't *try* to clear away all your thinking. And yet, you do commit yourself to the process by taking your time to meditate. These meditations will lead to a slowing of the relentless stream of thoughts until your consciousness has moments of stillness. Think of your mind as similar to a murky lake that becomes clear when the mud settles to the bottom. The potential for clarity is there in the lake, but the mud of thought is stirred up. All you need to do is allow your thoughts to settle. Look for moments between thoughts, and build from there. Throughout the process, you lessen the obstructiveness of thought so that inner calm emerges naturally. Paradoxically, by starting where you are and accepting what is there as you begin, you set the change process in motion. Between each thought in the rushing stream of thoughts, you can find an empty clearing. Fullness and emptiness are there together. Trust that the flow and the Tao of your inner nature will begin to emerge.

Exercise 7.1 Warming Up to No-Focus Meditation: Notice the Spaces Between

You are accustomed to thinking about the content of your thoughts and being swept along with them. But there are always moments between thoughts, subtle pauses. Empty space makes it possible to perceive anything. For the words on this page to be readable, there must be places without words, empty spaces, that allow the words to appear and their meaning to be revealed. Meditation brings out the hidden in what is evident.

You can find spaces everywhere. Even when you are in the midst of a manic or depressive episode, there are spaces between—subtle moments without symptoms. Learning to recognize empty space may help you to enlarge those healthy periods between symptoms for longer periods of stability.

Turn your attention to your face and notice your two eyes. Now, ask yourself, *How much space is there between my eyes?* Don't think of what's between your eyes; simply sense the literal distance between them. Meditate on that space between your eyes for a minute or so. Now, moving down through your body, ask yourself, *How far apart are my shoulders?* Think of that distance as an open, empty space. How far is it from your head to your toes? And what about the distance between where you are sitting and the wall? Empty spaces are always part of everything. Without the outside, there can be no inside. Look for the spaces now and meditate on them.

Exercise 7.2   Visualize Stillness for Clarity

In this exercise, use a peaceful visualization to slow down your mental chatter. Although we describe a scene in nature, feel free to use any peaceful place you prefer that is personally meaningful to you.

Sit quietly with your eyes closed. Imagine sitting on the shore of a pond that is alive with activity: frogs croak; crickets sing; birds fly overhead; a fish jumps out of the water, feeds on insects, splashes back in, and jumps out again in another spot after a bit. Wind whips over the water, stirring up the muddy bottom. All is movement. Then gradually, as the day passes, the conditions begin to shift. The wind dies down. The frogs settle in for a nap, the crickets are silent, the birds perch in the trees, and the fish stops jumping and waits. The pond is quiet. The murky, rippled surface calms as the mud sinks, leaving the water crystal clear. All is stillness. Imagine this scene vividly. Stay with the quiet, clear water.

Exercise 7.3   Clear Your Mind as You Walk

Begin with the mindfulness methods you practiced in chapter 6. Stand up and begin walking slowly, letting your arms swing naturally at your sides. Walk slowly, with awareness of every step. Pay attention to how your foot meets the ground. Notice how your weight shifts from foot to foot. Keep your breathing and your body relaxed as you walk slowly. Focus your attention on walking. If your mind starts to fill with thoughts about things other than walking, stop and wait as you return your mind to awareness of standing. Then, when your thoughts have returned to the present moment, begin walking again. Maintain awareness of every step with a quiet mind. Once you have become attuned to walking, let go of any focus on walking and just walk. Let your arms and legs move spontaneously, without thought. Allow yourself to be relaxed and natural as you move. When you feel ready to stop, stand for a minute or two, remaining open and aware in the moment.

Exercise 7.4　Classic Mind-Clearing Meditation

Meditation can bring about a slowing of thoughts until they literally stop, leaving a clear, calm consciousness. The instructions given here are drawn from the classic Zen instructions for zazen, a form of no-focus meditation. A famous Zen monk named Dogen wrote, "If you practice in this way for a long time, you will forget all attachments, and concentration will come naturally. This is Zazen" (Dumoulin 1988, 76).

Begin by doing this meditation for a few minutes. Then extend the time spent practicing as you are able to do so. If you find this difficult to do at first, don't be discouraged. Frequent practice for short intervals helps. Zazen is typically performed in a specific way. Therefore, we offer the complete set of instructions that are given when someone first begins this classic practice. Practice zazen as instructed if you can, but feel free to vary your body positioning as we described in chapter 4, in the section "The Sitting Posture," especially if you have any difficulties with sitting on the floor.

Set a thick pillow on the floor, and then add a second, smaller one on top. Sit down on the pillows and cross your legs. Place your hands on your lap, with your left hand on top of the middle joints of your right hand, with the middle fingers and thumbs lightly touching. Your hands will be shaped like an oval. One reason for crossing your legs and hands is to make the body a unity, with no distinction between left and right, no beginning and no end. Your mouth should be gently closed and your eyes half open, half closed. Do not focus your gaze on anything in particular. Remain relaxed but alert.

Keep your body straight, without leaning to one side or the other. Allow your spine to be straight. Relax your shoulders and keep your head straight, aligned in the center without tilting. Don't strain. Breathing passages should be free and unrestricted as your breathing becomes calm and steady. Begin by simply sitting and not thinking about anything in particular. If a thought or wish arises, bring it to awareness, noticing the wish or thought as it is. Don't evaluate it. Simply observe that it is, just as you did in the mindfulness meditations in chapter 6. Then allow the thought to leave, and return to not thinking about anything. In doing this, you will begin to become aware of both thinking and not thinking. Gradually, your thoughts will slow down a bit. Eventually your mind will clear, leaving a calm consciousness.

Exercise 7.5 Wu Wei: Indirect Mind Clearing

You probably have moments when you are doing things and not worrying about what you are doing. Even when you are experiencing bipolar symptoms, you have times when you might be watching a movie, reading a book, doing something you have done many times, or just standing in line, or you might even be in between activities, when your mind seems blank. You simply do what you do, accepting things as they are, without any pressures or concerns. At these moments, you tend to stop thinking about anything in particular. There is a natural inclination of the mind to be quiet and empty. You can use this natural tendency of mind to help build your skills for mind clearing. The next meditation follows wu wei, or letting be, and allows this built-in tendency to help you. As the great Zen master Shunryu Suzuki (1970, 33) explained, "The purpose is to see things as they are, to observe things as they are, and to let everything go as it goes. This is to put everything under control in its widest sense."

Pick a time when you have no immediate responsibilities or obligations, and therefore less need for activity. You might find that right before sleep or first thing in the morning is a good time, or during a lunch break or at a time when you are alone and nothing has to be done. Another possibility is to find a time when your attention wants to drift or your mind feels blank. At moments like these, you might try to force yourself to do a chore or task, to become active. But instead, use that moment as an opportunity to try this exercise.

Spend a few minutes permitting your mind to be blank, and explore how expansive that blankness can be. Don't try to discern what it is exactly; just let this spontaneous tendency be, and do nothing. These open moments of mind may happen while you are sitting, standing, or even waiting in line at the store. The important thing is to notice the moment's opportunity, and when circumstances permit, let the experience take place.

Let your thoughts drift. Don't do anything and don't think about anything in particular. Simply sit quietly, allowing this experience to develop. Let your breathing be comfortable and allow your body to relax. After allowing the naturally occurring blankness to be there, even if only for a brief time, you may find that you can deliberately access this mental quiet at other times as well. Do the other exercises in this chapter again. You might find them easier to do.

Conclusion

Practice the meditations in this chapter and the previous two chapters until you feel comfortable with them. Be encouraged when you feel that you were able to do a meditation well, but don't worry when a meditation seems too difficult for you. We have offered many different options. Some will be easier for you to do than others, and that's normal.

You may begin to sense some movement toward balance. The effects are subtle at first. Part 3 shows you how to apply these meditations and variations of them to help you with your difficulties. We encourage you to keep practicing and enjoy the process! All of these skills will help you in part 3, when you address your problems and learn how to apply these methods to discover your optimal balance and ways to maintain it for a fulfilling, happy life.

Easing Your Moods, Fulfilling Your Talents

Chapter 8

The Way Out of Stress

We have all heard someone say, "I'm stressed!" And you have probably even said it yourself. Everyone has moments of feeling stressed, because the stress reaction is built into the nervous system. Stress is the body's response to a threat or demand. It's a helpful response in that it activates your body to take action against danger. But the response becomes a problem when your body remains activated even when there is no real need to be on alert. Even though stress is something everyone has to deal with, it may be even more challenging for you if you are bipolar. This is because those who have bipolar disorder tend to react more strongly to stress than do other people. In fact, stress can trigger a manic or depressive mood.

You might think that stress comes only from threats or negative events. But positive things such as the birth of a child, graduating from college, or planning a wedding can also be stressful. The founder of stress theory, Hans Selye (1975), called the positive kind of stress *eustress*. Eustress helps to explain why you may have had a strong mood shift after very positive experiences as well as negative ones. Eustress can be beneficial if managed well.

This chapter will help you learn how stress affects you. You will learn about your nervous system's natural mechanisms for coping with stress and how to use these mechanisms for your benefit. We describe some of the research findings about stress and bipolar disorder, plus provide research on how meditation reduces stress. We give you some meditations to help you ease your stress reaction and handle stressful situations better. You will also learn how being more mindful and less judgmental will lessen your discomfort, calm your nervous system when it is overactivated, and enhance your strengths to handle stress better and enjoy some stress-free moments. We encourage you to use the meditations in this chapter regularly at any time, but especially when life becomes stressful. You can also use meditations from other chapters.

Research Findings about Stress and Bipolar Disorder

The symptoms of bipolar disorder can stress your mind, brain, and body. In general, the burden of stress can make you feel more uncomfortable. Many kinds of difficult events in your life can trigger a bipolar episode. Kay Redfield Jamison, a noted psychologist and author who is also a bipolar sufferer, found a high correlation between stressful life events and relapse, even when the outpatients she tested were taking their medications and following their treatment regimens (Ellicott et al. 1990). More recently, researchers found that stressful events in your life, either negative or positive, may trigger an episode. Certain abnormalities in the body's stress pathway were shown to have an influence on whether people had a depressive or manic cycle. Researchers proposed that altering the stress pathway could have helpful therapeutic effects on bipolar disorder (Daban et al. 2005). Meditation helps calm an overactivated stress pathway, thus offering a helpful treatment.

So, although stress is not the only cause of bipolar episodes and bipolar disorder is not defined as simply a stress disorder, it certainly makes sense for you to lower your stress levels. Learning how to reduce stress and handle it well is a good place to start in lessening your bipolar reactions. And being able to handle stress better may even help you to have fewer bipolar episodes. We have found that when our clients learned how to manage stress better, they had fewer episodes and an easier time lessening their mood swings. Their distress lost its sting.

People vary widely in how they respond to the challenges in their lives. You can learn how to ease your feelings of stress and meet challenges better with strength, confidence, and balance. Paradoxically, stress can become positive. We begin part 3 with meditations for stress.

Stress and Balance

Stress comes from some demand outside of you, such as in your environment, or from some problem within you, such as an illness, that alters the balance of your nervous system. Eastern healing has a similar idea: the organs of your body respond to the yin and yang forces of nature found in the environment, or to internal imbalances of chi (Ming 2001). So, according to both Eastern and Western medical traditions, your body is responsive to the challenges of life. Your nervous system reacts by becoming activated in order to meet the challenge. When the difficulty has passed, the nervous system deactivates, bringing you back into balance. This activating and deactivating is like a continuously balancing equation. You are always responding to these forces as you go through life.

Hippocrates, the ancient Greek founder of Western medicine, recognized that the body has an innate capacity to return to balance when it has been thrown off, through its natural ability to heal. Walter Cannon (1871 to 1945), a professor of physiology at Harvard University, gave the name *homeostasis* to this natural wisdom of the body to return to balance. He believed that when natural balance is disturbed, such as from being stressed, the body instinctively tries to return to homeostatic stability. For example, after you have made an intense effort, such as working long hours on something, you will feel tired and want to rest. When everything functions as it should, you will tend to act in a natural way: eat when you are hungry and sleep when you are tired. But when you have mood problems, you may lose touch with your natural instincts for healthy eating and sleeping, which adds extra stress.

The way you react to stress is built right into your nervous system. Several brain systems that have a strong connection to thoughts and feelings link up with your peripheral nervous system. On the neurobiological level, this *stress reaction*, as it is called, comes from the body's natural fear response, which helps you to protect yourself from threatening situations.

The Anatomy of a Stress Reaction

Your nervous system consists of your brain and spinal cord, plus a peripheral nervous system with a set of nerves that extend throughout your entire body. This peripheral nervous system has two main parts: the sympathetic nervous system (SNS) and the parasympathetic nervous system (PNS). The SNS helps activate you to respond to the world and meet the demands of life, whatever they might be. It is activated at any time, day or night, as you address your tasks, whatever they may be. The PNS helps you to relax after the need for effort has passed. So, built right into your physiology is a natural balancing system that helps you to be alert when needed and then to calm down when the stress has passed. You can draw on this tendency toward balance to help you ease your moods.

Under threat, these two systems are protective, helping you to meet a challenge by either getting away from it, fighting against it, or quietly waiting without moving, known as "flight, fight, or freeze." The SNS is activated to help you take an immediate action, such as jumping out of the way of a speeding car that's coming toward you. Your heart rate increases, and your breathing quickens. These changes make it easier for you to move quickly, without any hesitation. After the threat has passed, your PNS brings you back to rest by slowing down your breathing and lowering your heart rate. This balancing between the SNS to activate and the PNS to calm is a normal, protective response to threat. But if you have bipolar disorder, the nervous system remains activated. Sustained activation, without times of calm and rest, leads to your system becoming depleted. The result is that you feel negatively stressed.

Now let's look a little closer at what is actually occurring, first, during a normal stress reaction and, then, when you are having a bipolar mood swing. Normally, a feedback loop known as the *hypothalamic-pituitary-adrenal axis* (HPA axis, also known as the "fear-stress pathway") directs the SNS and PNS changes, becoming activated when you feel threatened and staying activated when you are under continual stress. The reaction involves an interaction between your brain and nervous system with the hormones in your endocrine system. The hypothalamus receives signals related to what you are sensing in your body and what you are experiencing in the environment. The hypothalamus then releases neurotransmitters and hormones that raise the levels of the stress hormone *cortisol*, which is routed quickly into your bloodstream for a fast response. In healthy individuals, when the stress has passed, the HPA axis deactivates and lowers the activation in the nervous system. Thus the HPA pathway is important in maintaining balance between your body and the environment.

But when you have strong mood swings, your HPA pathway remains continuously activated. Researchers found that people who suffer from mood disorders have chronic hyperactivity in the HPA pathway, thus keeping the SNS overactivated (Daban et al. 2005). You experience this activation as stressful, similar to revving your car engine even when the gear is in neutral.

Thus, a stress reaction adds extra discomfort to your moods. The positive side is that by lessening your stress, like turning down the idle in your car's motor, you create a more comfortable and efficient balance, even if you are having a strong mood. The nonspecific calming and improved coping ability that result will help ease your moody reactions. Meditation enlists your body's natural tendency to restore balance, thereby helping to relieve your stress.

Tracking Your Stress Patterns

You can recognize some of the signs of stress that occur when your stress pathway remains activated. Use the following stress-symptom checklists to track the changes that occur in your body, emotions, and behavior. As you come to recognize that you are stressed, you can do the meditations in this chapter to help reduce your stress levels and return your HPA pathway to balance. Check off the symptoms that you notice when you are feeling stressed, using the following physical, emotional, and behavioral checklists. Then move on to the meditation that follows all three checklists.

Checklist of Physical Symptoms

- [ ] Dry mouth
- [ ] Excessive sweating

- [ ] Frequent illnesses
- [ ] Gastrointestinal problems
- [x] Teeth grinding
- [x] Headaches
- [x] Raised blood pressure
- [x] Pounding heart
- [ ] Stiff neck or sore lower back

Checklist of Emotional Symptoms

- [x] Anxiety
- [ ] Chronic tiredness
- [ ] Easily startled
- [x] Impulsiveness
- [x] Difficulty concentrating
- [x] Irritability
- [x] Trouble remembering things

Checklist of Behavioral Symptoms

- [x] Crying
- [ ] A change in your eating habits
- [x] Disrupted sleeping patterns
- [x] Impatience
- [x] Trouble communicating
- [ ] Avoidance of friends and family
- [x] Increased use of drugs, alcohol, or tobacco

Exercise 8.1   Focus on Sensing a Stress Reaction as It Happens

A natural reaction to stress takes place automatically, but you can deliberately focus your attention in order to notice the signs. Use the focus and open-focus meditations you learned in chapters 5 and 6. Turn your attention to your process of experiencing after a minor stressful event, such as an argument at home or a work demand. Review the previous three checklists you filled out. Then, notice the details of your physical, emotional, and behavioral symptoms that you marked on your checklists. These are the characteristic experiences you have when you are under stress. Observe the sensations just as they are, such as by noticing sweating in your palms or burning in your stomach. Notice your emotions, such as fear or worry. And note any typical behaviors, such as staying up late or increased drug use. Get to know these characteristic reactions to stress, which will serve as signposts alerting you to take some action to alleviate your stress. Transform a negative reaction to stress into a positive reaction.

Research on Meditation for Stress

Meditation has been researched for many decades as a viable method for rebalancing the nervous system and reducing the harmful effects of excess stress. Herbert Benson was one of the earliest researchers on the health benefits of meditation as a stress-reduction method. He formulated a generic meditation method he called the *relaxation response* (Benson 1975). Meditations that teach you to follow your breath and quiet your thoughts can stimulate a relaxation response. Some of Benson's early studies (see, for example, Benson et al. 1974) showed that meditation could lower elevated blood pressure, which is one of the symptoms of stress, and by doing so, people felt less stressed.

Daniel Goleman also did some early studies testing how meditation reduces stress. In one experiment, he showed subjects a stressful movie and found that meditators had fewer stress reactions than nonmeditators (Goleman and Schwartz 1976). In another study, eighty students were divided into two groups. The experimental group meditated for twenty minutes once a day for five days, whereas the control group did not. After meditation the experimental group had measurably less anxiety and lower levels of cortisol, the stress hormone. Levels of anxiety, depression, anger, and fatigue also decreased (Tang et. al 2007).

Many different research groups have studied the effects of various types of meditation on reducing stress, such as Michael Dillbeck and colleagues (1986) using Transcendental Meditation (TM), and Jon Kabat-Zinn, who developed the Mindfulness-Based Stress Reduction (MBSR) program, which is widely used in psychotherapy today (Miller, Fletcher, and Kabat-Zinn 1995). The research projects mentioned here are just a few selections from the many studies that show how helpful meditation is for reducing stress.

Reducing Stress

Maria had always been a harsh critic of life, especially when she was in her depressed cycle. She experienced each work or home responsibility as a stressor. She said that she had been dealt a bad hand, and complained bitterly about how stressful her life was. Now middle-aged, she felt doomed to more of the same, without any hope of experiencing something better. Whenever she got started, her thoughts gained momentum, hurling her into a dangerously dark emotional place. She felt out of control of her life.

We introduced her to a series of meditations that taught her how to notice what she was feeling, but with a difference. Instead of spending her time thinking how stressful things were, she was trained to simply notice what she was experiencing. At first, she had trouble recognizing when she was making a judgment. But in time, she could distinguish observing from judging. She began to notice that negative feelings seemed to follow her negative judgments. Through regular practice of nonjudgmental awareness, Maria became more objective. She stopped being so critical of her life experiences. She enjoyed having some positive moments during meditation. And as a result, she discovered some bright spots in her life. She could see some areas of her life that she wanted to change, and she learned to accept more gracefully what she could not change. The transformation was remarkable. She discovered a surprising use for her talent for critical thinking! Now that her judging ability was freed, she redirected it into learning philosophy, where thinking critically is highly prized. Her fluid associative capability became positive when linked to reason.

How you interpret and handle the stressors in your life has a big influence on how stressed you feel. Research on stress has found that when people can observe without adding a secondary layer of negative judgment, they cope better (Janis 1971). So, deepening your perception of the stress you are experiencing, without judging it as good or bad, and instead simply attuning to the Tao of your stress as it is, will help you be less stressed. Mindfulness meditation begins with noticing the flow of what you are experiencing right now, which makes it a helpful way to gain an accurate and deeper perception of what's really going on. If you are feeling stressed, you can use your new mindfulness skills to gain insight that will help you to cope better and lessen the reaction.

Recall that attuning to the way something is, its Tao, will help you to understand it better. Carefully observing what you are experiencing is the best place to start when you are working with stress patterns. Initiate a change process where you are, and study it well. Thus, if you are feeling stressed right now, you don't have to try to make yourself feel something else in order to change it. Begin noticing what you are experiencing as you experience it, and change will flow automatically as you get more in touch with what you experience. In that way, you will be able to recognize what you tend to do that makes things harder. In addition, you can learn how to nurture your built-in abilities to cope well and give yourself what you need.

Focus Meditations for Getting in Touch

The two meditations that follow will help you to get in touch with what's happening around you and then what's occurring within you. By becoming aware, you inject a new, healing perspective into the situation that changes it. Practice these two meditations in sequence. Repeat them at different times and in different places.

Exercise 8.2 Focus on Outer Experiencing

Begin by focusing your attention on the many details of what you experience in your environment. Practice this meditation today for a few minutes and then do the next meditation.

Find a comfortable place to sit down, and take a moment to just sit quietly. Then, turn your attention outward, to the place where you are sitting right now. If you are in a room in your house, notice what's around you in this room. If you are outside, pay attention to what you perceive right there in your immediate surroundings. Observe the sounds, the things in your view, the surface you are sitting on, the temperature of the air around you, and anything else that you hear, see, smell, or touch. If it's helpful, begin each observation by thinking, *Now I notice* _____ or *Now I am aware of* _____ , filling in what you perceive. Pay close attention to whatever you perceive in your immediate environment. Keep your observations concrete. Keep following your observations of your surroundings for several minutes, up to five minutes.

Exercise 8.3 Focus on Inner Experiencing

After doing the previous meditation, turn the focus of your attention inward. Notice your heartbeat, body temperature, or anything else that is happening internally. Once again, say to yourself, *Now I am aware of* _____ , filling in what you notice, if this helps you to stay attuned to what you sense within. As you continue in this way, you may perceive something different in the next moment, so don't assume that the next moment will be the same as the last one. Keep your observations objective by simply observing the sensations that you are experiencing during the meditation.

Alternate the focus of your attention between your outer and inner surroundings, even for a few minutes, at different times during the day. These meditations have a centering effect. You will get more in touch with what you are experiencing, which will enable you to handle whatever is happening more calmly and realistically. Practicing these two meditations regularly will develop your self-awareness, which will help lower activation of your nervous system so that you can better address stressful situations.

Stepping Away from Negative Judgments

The next exercise moves you away from negative judgments you might be making about feeling stressed. Being able to let go of your critical assessments can make space for something more constructive.

Exercise 8.4 Clear and Open in the Moment

For this no-focus meditation, you can foster an experience within yourself that is free of judging, open, and empty in the moment. Do this meditation often, especially when you are feeling stressed.

Sit or stand wherever you are, and clear your mind of any thoughts. Maintain a nonjudgmental attitude, as you practiced in chapter 6. So, if a judgmental thought appears, such as how terrible your stress is, notice that you are making this judgment. Then, let it go for now and return to your clear, centered moment, here and now. Keep doing so with each intruding thought. In time, your thoughts slow and you will experience moments of calm. In this open place, there is no stress. Sit quietly in this way, allowing yourself to enjoy a few minutes of peace.

When you feel ready to stop, yawn and stretch as you stand up and move around a bit. You may also feel a certain amount of relief, having cleared your mind for just a few moments. If you find that you had difficulty letting go of harsh judgments or intruding thoughts, turn to chapter 9 and do the meditations on thinking, which will help you alter negative patterns of thought. Then you may find that your stressful situation becomes more manageable.

Allowing Relaxation with Breathing

Relaxation is a helpful component of stress reduction. Since breathing is one of the most direct links to your internal body reactions, you can greatly reduce your stress by turning your attention to your breathing. The following is a way to focus your attention on visualizing calm and relaxation. You may find this helpful in bringing you some temporary relief when you are in the midst of a stressful situation. Take frequent short breaks to relax with meditation. Meditate intermittently during each day for a stronger effect.

Exercise 8.5   Focus on Visualizing Relaxed Breathing

Just focusing your attention on breathing tends to have an overall calming effect. Practice the breathing meditations from chapter 5 to reduce your stress. In addition, try this breathing visualization for another variation of focus on breathing.

Lie on your back, with your knees drawn up and your feet flat on the floor. Close your eyes and allow your breathing to be relaxed. With each breath in, imagine that you are drawing in cleansing, fresh air; and with each breath out, imagine that the tension in your muscles begins to ease. You might like to visualize the air in different colors for the in- and out-breaths, for example, white or yellow air on the in-breath, and brown or red air on the out-breath, but feel free to pick any colors that come to mind. Focus your breathing on any particular muscle group that feels tight. Visualize the air as you inhale, bringing a refreshing coolness to that area. Then as you exhale, visualize these muscles relaxing a bit. Allow your muscles to loosen as they naturally do, but don't force any change. Rest comfortably for five minutes or so, breathing out lightly to disperse tightness. When you feel ready, sit up and stretch.

Now that you have experienced being more relaxed, you can recognize the difference between feeling relaxed and feeling tense. If you notice yourself feeling tense, use breathing meditations. You will set a calmer pattern in motion the more often you practice these relaxing meditations. Your nervous system calms down so that less of the stress hormone cortisol is released. With a calmer nervous system, you will feel more relaxed and at ease.

Creating a Meditative Stress Sanctuary

When your stress reaction doesn't ease, another use of meditation is to fill your mind with something different.

As we discussed earlier in this chapter, your nervous system can help you face stressful situations, and then the nervous system returns to a calmer, less-activated level when the stress has passed. But if you have been through something traumatic, such as a bipolar episode, your nervous system may remain overactivated, leaving you on edge. Using meditation, you can signal your nervous system to restore its balance naturally. You can do this by creating an oasis of relief, a kind of sanctuary that is safe and comfortable, and that encourages your brain-body pathways to regain balance. Researchers found that meditation practice makes this interlude possible. Skilled meditators can create a peaceful moment no matter what mood they were in before meditating (Kohr 1977).

Gary was diagnosed with bipolar disorder during his college years. He feared his severe mood swings and worried that he wouldn't be able to finish college. We taught him meditation, which he enjoyed. But whenever he was under stress from the demands of school, his moods began to swing. We asked him, "Where do you feel most comfortable?" Having been raised in San Diego, he answered, as many young people do who grow up here, near the ocean, "Surfing at the beach!" We encouraged him to use as his sanctuary a visualization of himself surfing. He imagined the rise and fall of the waves, and how he could stay balanced and in control on his board while riding the highs and lows. He returned to this sanctuary in meditation whenever he felt overstressed, and was able to ride the waves of his moods and eventually graduate from college.

Exercise 8.6 Find Your Sanctuary

Find a comfortable sitting or lying-down position for meditation in a place where you won't be interrupted. Visualize a place where you feel safe, happy, and comfortable. It could be a real place where you have been sometime in your life or a fantasy place that you create. It could be outdoors in nature or indoors in a safe, well-fortified location. Use your own responses of relaxation and comfort as your guide for choosing.

Once you have decided on a place, begin to vividly imagine it. What do you see? If it's a garden, look at the flowers. Look up at the sky and observe any clouds. What colors do you see? Look down at the ground and out beyond the horizon. Imagine that you explore a winding path, perhaps with soft cushioning under each step you take. Do you hear birds singing or the rustling of leaves from a gentle breeze? Imagine the fragrance from the flowers and grass. Call on all your senses to vividly create this experience of your sanctuary place.

Take some time each day, especially when you are working on reducing your stress, to return to this place.

Shifting from Here to There

Whenever you notice yourself feeling uncomfortable, fill out the stress-symptom checklists from earlier in this chapter. If you are stressed, use the meditations in this chapter to help you to lower your stress level. You can use one of the earlier relaxation meditations, go to your meditation sanctuary, or just take a relaxing moment. After you feel calmer, pay attention to your inner experiencing, mindfully noticing whatever you can in your breathing, heartbeat, muscles, and stomach.

Shift your attention back and forth between the two different experiences. Can you discern any differences in your inner experiencing between when you were thinking about the stressful events and when you were just relaxing? People often find that certain muscles tense in a particular pattern, such as around the neck or shoulders. Another common effect is that the breathing rate quickens as thoughts turn negative. Doing the series of meditations in this chapter at different times will help you to discern characteristic stress patterns that can serve as clues for when you are starting to feel stressed. As soon as you notice this happening, take some time, even a few minutes here and there, to do the relaxing and calming meditations provided throughout this book. Approach the stressor mindfully, without making it worse with negative judgments. You will feel better if you lessen your stress to a manageable level when things get tough.

Building Your Capacities

As you become more relaxed and centered, you will be better able to foster your potential to handle stressful situations. This exercise draws on abilities you already have and expands them. Repeat this exercise at different times and over several days.

Exercise 8.7   Visualize Your Strengths

You can build your inner strength to handle stressful situations better by using some resources you have used successfully in the past. Vividly imagine taking appropriate action with a situation that you can realistically affect. For example, even if you worry that your stress is overwhelming, you can probably recall a time when you met a small challenge and handled it well. Vividly remember what you did to overcome that difficulty. Now, imagine yourself successfully applying this same strategy to a more demanding situation. Vividly picture yourself handling your stressful event competently. Invite the image to become clearer, enlisting all of your senses. Be patient as you relax into the experience, and wait for your response. Don't try to force anything to happen. Simply imagine yourself succeeding, and then wait as you allow the experience to unfold by wu wei, the way of nonaction.

Conclusion

The HPA pathway helps you meet challenges and then return to balance. If your nervous system remains overactivated, you may become more vulnerable to a bipolar episode. Reducing your stress levels can not only resolve discomforts, but also keep your moods in balance, making your life flow more smoothly and comfortably. Begin the process by using mindfulness meditations to become more aware of your typical reaction to stress and aware of its Tao. You gain even more control of your reactions as you learn to stop judging yourself, your situation, and other people in your life. The real source of balance is within you. Meditation gives you a path to follow that leads you right to that source within, where you are stress free, where you can find your inner peace and always call on it whenever you need to. Meditate regularly at various times throughout the day. The effects will deepen and spread.

Chapter 9

Moderate Your Depression

You have probably suffered the discomfort of depression, the part of the bipolar cycle that most people find challenging. Neurochemical changes are occurring at the synapses when you feel depressed, euphoric, or under stress. The action of two neurotransmitters, *norepinephrine* and *serotonin*, is disrupted. Norepinephrine is important for arousal and attention. Serotonin is involved in mood, pain, aggression, and sleep. The medications you take may help to normalize the activity at the synapses by altering the balance of neurotransmitters (Duman 2002). For example, taking lithium helps to even out your mood swings and lessen your depressed mood, because lithium acts on serotonin and norepinephrine as well as *dopamine*, the neurotransmitter associated with feelings of enjoyment. Meditation does this too.

Modern research has found that part of what makes you feel depressed is caused not only by your neurochemistry, but also by how you think. So, you may continue to feel depressed even though you take your medication. According to cognitive theories of depression, your own faulty attitudes and negative views of yourself are underlying causes that make the symptoms and neurological reactions more pronounced (Abela and D'Alessandro 2002). In addition, your loss of energy reflects lower activation of your nervous system. Recent studies have shown that meditation combined with cognitive therapy is most helpful for overcoming depression (Barnhofer et al. 2009) and preventing it from recurring (Williams and Kuyken 2012). Thus, therapeutic methods that change how you think and meditations to help energize your nervous system, when combined with your medication, can help you to overcome your depression.

This chapter will guide you in a meditative way to recognize what you are thinking when you are depressed, and to learn how to change the thought patterns that may be making you feel worse. You will apply the methods that you learned in part 2 to clarify your thinking. Meditation can also raise your energy levels for a healthier balance, and the second half of the chapter offers helpful methods for activating your chi.

At first you may sometimes have difficulty in bringing yourself to meditate when you feel depressed. This is normal, especially when you are feeling low. Begin by doing short meditations more often. Even one minute can be helpful. Don't expect instant results. After all, medications take time to have an effect, and similarly, you should give your meditation practice the time needed to alter your nervous system, shift entrenched thought patterns, and raise your energy levels.

The Thinking Component of Depression

Depression has long been linked to certain kinds of thoughts. The famous founder of psychoanalysis, Sigmund Freud (1856 to 1939), described melancholia (his word for depression) as a punishing, harsh criticism toward the ego: "If we turn to melancholia first, we find that the excessively strong super ego, which has obtained a hold on consciousness, rages against the ego with merciless violence" (Freud [1923] 1961, 43). Modern cognitive psychotherapies point out that such harsh personal assessments are irrational. By holding on to irrational beliefs, you make yourself miserable (Ellis and Ellis 2011). What you think literally affects how you feel.

Changing what you think is not just a matter of talking yourself out of feeling critical or just deciding to feel good. All of those broken New Year's resolutions are evidence that simply resolving to be different is usually ineffective. Real change requires an inner transformation.

Meditation elicits a lasting alteration in your thinking that draws on and enhances your better qualities. As you clear away negative thought patterns, you open the way for something new.

When you are feeling depressed, you may truly believe that everything is dark. But the Tao suggests another possibility. The Tao manifests in the world as yin and yang, the two opposites. This wisdom is applicable to thinking as well. Even though your dark mood may feel pervasive, the seeds for a bit of brightness are also present. You can uncover that faint ray of hope within the vast darkness and nurture it. Then it will grow.

The Power of Thought: The Ideomotor Mind-Body Link

Thoughts have a tremendous influence on what you feel, all the way down to the physiological level, because there is a fundamental link between your thoughts and your body. The ideomotor link (introduced in chapter 4 in the "Honing Your Meditation Tools" section) was discovered many years ago and described by William James (1842 to 1910), the American father of psychology. This ideomotor link occurs naturally when a thought, image, or experience is automatically translated into body experience, movement, or sensation.

The ideomotor link can help you to feel less depressed. But, when you engage in negative thinking, you may be eliciting some of the characteristic sensations of depression, such as feeling sluggish, uncomfortable, or sad due to the ideomotor link between mind and body. Change your negative patterns of thinking, and you lessen your body discomfort. Imaging the positive and your body responds.

Four Steps to Altering Your Thinking

The following are four steps for working with any of your thinking patterns that may be eliciting a negative ideomotor reaction:

1. Observe.

2. Question.

3. Imagine.

4. Allow.

Each of these steps engages meditative focus in a different way. You will be better equipped to transform your unrealistic and inaccurate thoughts that generate overly negative thinking, and allow change to automatically take place. Apply some diligence at first to set the process in motion. Once the process has begun, change will flow naturally. As you attune to your multisided Tao, the positive and negative are put into a more realistic balance.

Step One: Observe

When you sit quietly, closing your eyes, you probably notice your thoughts as they flow by. For example, you might notice that you are dwelling on something that was said to you or perhaps ruminating about how terrible you feel. You might notice some kind of assertion that you are making, such as *My loved one shouldn't talk to me that way*, *Why does this always happen to me?*, or even *I'm such a mess*. You are likely to notice different thoughts at different times of the day or night. The first step begins with mindful awareness to bring you in touch with the Tao of your thinking.

Exercise 9.1   Patterns of Thoughts

As you observe your thinking at different times, you begin to notice distinct patterns of thoughts emerging. Typically when people are depressed, their thoughts form these kinds of patterns:

- Self-critical

- Self-castigating

- Self-blaming

- Helpless and hopeless

Recognizing these typical thought patterns is the next step in altering your depressed mood. The following parts of this exercise help you to recognize and work with your typical thought patterns.

Read about all four patterns. Do mindful awareness of your thinking several times, noting thoughts until you have identified some of your typical thoughts. Match them to one of the four patterns. Once you have identified your pattern, apply the nonjudgmental awareness that you practiced in chapter 6. This means noticing the pattern of thinking, but not taking that second step of thinking *This is terrible, I shouldn't be thinking that*, or *Of course, I'm thinking that, because it's right*. Simply observe and trust that later exercises in this chapter will help you deal with those secondary judgments too.

Self-Criticism

Self-criticism is one of the most typical thinking patterns in people who are feeling depressed. Do you observe that you typically have critical thoughts about yourself? Are you thinking that you are a failure? Do you think you are wasting your life? Perhaps you are criticizing yourself for having spent too much money. Notice these thoughts, especially those that repeat. Remain observant and steady as you meditate. Mindful awareness sets the healing process in motion.

Self-Castigation

Perhaps your thoughts are self-punitive. You might be thinking things like *I deserve all the bad things that happen to me*. Maybe when you don't quite feel like caring for yourself properly, such as when you are not eating or sleeping, you are saying to yourself, *I don't deserve to be cared for*. Or maybe you are thinking, *I don't merit feeling good.* Once again, notice these thoughts without adding to them by judging them as good or bad. Just notice, remaining calm in your meditation and trusting that this observation is the step toward altering your depressed mood.

Self-Blame

Another common type of thinking that people have when they are depressed is blaming themselves. For example, perhaps someone spoke harshly to you or seemed to ignore you. Your reaction might be to think, *It's my fault.* Thinking this way, you might begin to feel angry at yourself. Notice whether you are blaming yourself for situations in your life. Listen to internal phrases like *I made her say that* or perhaps *If it weren't for me, that wouldn't have happened.* Here again, notice these thoughts mindfully, without assessing them as right or wrong. Be patient and trust the process.

Helplessness and Hopelessness

Another pervasive reaction pattern is to feel helpless. Psychologist Martin Seligman performed a groundbreaking experiment in 1967 that opened a new way to understand depression (Seligman and Maier 1967). The experiment put three groups of dogs in harnesses to prevent them from escaping. One group was simply harnessed for a time. A second group got a shock but could press a lever to stop the shock. For the third group, pressing the lever did not stop the shock. Later, all three groups were shocked but also were offered the opportunity to run away by jumping over a low barrier. Seligman expected that all the dogs would escape the shock, and the first two groups did just that. But the third group had a different reaction. They seemed to have learned that nothing they did would help, so they just lay down helplessly and whimpered. Seligman believed that this helpless reaction was similar to depression.

Pay attention to your thoughts mindfully. Do you notice yourself thinking, *There's nothing I can do, I feel helpless,* or maybe *Nothing I do is ever right?* If you notice these kinds of thoughts, you may be feeling helpless and hopeless. Observe these thoughts now, without judging them as good or bad. Trust that by becoming aware that you are having thoughts of helplessness, you have taken the first step in making a change.

Step Two: Question

Instead of simply accepting your critical, negative thought patterns as true, question them. Each pattern has an inherent flaw, something illogical or irrational. To uncover the faults in your thinking, rephrase your thought as a question. For example, if you are having the self-critical thought that your life is a failure, ask yourself, *Is every aspect of my life a failure?* The likelihood is that, like most people, you have some failures but also some successes.

We have found that even our most depressed clients are able to find something that they do well. For example, Jeremy had lost his job, his wife, and custody of his child after a series of manic episodes over several years. The depression that followed these stressful events was much deeper and more disturbing than ever before. He told us, "I have failed in every aspect of my life." We invited him to question that general statement and look for some successes. At first he could think of nothing he had done right. But then he thought of the achievement of his daughter, who showed exceptional talent in science. She had won first place at her sixth-grade science fair. Humbly, he admitted, "I gave her life! So I did something right! Maybe she will save the world someday." Eventually he came to realize that he had been a good father at times, especially when he wasn't in the middle of a bipolar episode. He felt inspired to make a greater effort to stabilize his moods for the sake of his daughter.

Question the patterns you have uncovered. The following are some typical flaws that can help you to counteract the negative thinking patterns that often go with depression.

Generalizing

One of the most common flaws in all four of the thought patterns is generalizing. Jeremy was generalizing when he told himself that his whole life was a failure. If you notice yourself internally describing a fault of yours in terms of all, every, always, or never, consider this to be an alert

125

that you are generalizing. Life is full of diversity. One situation is not the same as another. If you group things into one general category, you miss the nuances, the yin within the yang. You are always more than any single generalization. Question such assumptions and look for the exceptions.

Circular Thinking

Often the thinking you do when you are depressed runs in a circle. Nan went through this set of thoughts: *I'm depressed because I'm so low on money. But I can't go to work today because I'm so depressed.* This example of circular thinking prevented Nan from changing her situation. Nan knew she was depressed, so she felt that she couldn't question that fact. But she did question whether her depression was simply based on lack of money. She began to realize that she used money as an excuse. Of course, she wished she made more money, but what really mattered was her family. As she paid attention to what they were saying to her, she could see that they loved her and were concerned about her suffering.

You may be trapped in a thought circle. If so, notice it and begin to question how irrational it is to lock yourself into a circular argument. Look beyond the obvious, as Nan did, to find your way out of circular thinking.

Mistaking the Ideal for the Real

Having ideals for yourself can give you something to strive toward. Goals are helpful for steering your life in a positive direction. But often, self-criticism and self-castigation come from expecting that you should be your ideal, and then feeling angry when you don't seem to measure up.

Tad had landed a midlevel position at a large company right out of college. At first, he was elated to be hired by such a renowned company, but gradually he became depressed. He told himself that because he was not as successful as the CEO of the company, he was no good. He spent much of his time thinking of all the ways in which he was incompetent because he hadn't met his goal of becoming a CEO. Tad ignored the fact that the CEO was twice his age and had worked his way up from humble beginnings. With his attention directed at the negative, Tad overlooked the times when he did something worthwhile. He was a capable and skilled person who often produced quality work. But to him, his achievements were always flawed. When we pointed out an accomplishment, he would say, "I could have done it better," or "It's incomplete; there's more to do." As his depression grew deeper, his work suffered. What helped Tad turn his mood around was recognizing the difference between the ideal he had for himself and the real situation he was in.

What do you expect for yourself? What are your ideals? Are they reasonable goals, or are they out of reach? Do you compare yourself to standards that are beyond you, and then criticize yourself for not meeting them? Question these ideals. Distinguish between having an inspiring ideal and accepting what's real for you now.

Exercise 9.2   Focus on Activity Itself

You have begun to question your faulty thinking. Now, focus your attention on what you are doing as you do it. This meditation uses the general method of focusing your attention that was taught in chapter 5. First, do this exercise when you are taking on a typical task. Later, complete the exercise when you are doing a task for work or something that you are trying to accomplish that may be challenging.

Before you begin to perform the task, sit quietly and focus your attention on your breathing. You can review the exercises in chapter 5 first or just proceed directly with this exercise. Allow your attention to remain focused on breathing naturally for several minutes.

Now, begin to perform the task. Suppose you chose to wash the car. (Please feel free to choose any household task you regularly perform.) Pay close attention as you wet down the car. Watch the water spray on each area. Keep your attention focused on the water as it flows over the car. Notice the temperature of the water and how it looks as the car becomes wet. When you are soaping the car, pay close attention to the consistency of the soap and any aromas you smell. Feel the contours of the car as you soap the surface and sense the slippery suds, while keeping all your attention focused on just soaping. When you are ready, rinse the car, carefully attending to the spray of the water. Watch the soap slide off the car, keeping your attention directed to rinsing. Finally, dry the car. Pay attention to the soft cloth, working carefully all around the surface. Keep your attention focused on each action, one at a time. If, at any point, you find yourself thinking about something else, stop, return your attention to your breathing for a moment, and then, when you feel centered in the present moment, go back to washing the car. When you have finished, take several moments to appreciate your accomplishment.

When you are working on something that you are trying to achieve, turn your attention to it, just as you did the previous task, such as washing the car. Rather than putting the focus of your attention on what's wrong, what you aren't doing, or how hard it is, simply pay attention to each step of what you are doing as you do it. So, if you are writing a report, notice how your fingers strike the keys of the computer, and look at the screen and see the data as it appears. Think about the content of what you are trying to do. Whenever you catch yourself derogating yourself or judging your abilities, gently return to the task itself. With your meditative focus, you will find yourself noticing important details that you might usually miss. You will do a more complete and careful job, which often leads to greater success overall.

Step Three: Imagine

Now that you have begun to clarify your thought patterns, questioned their irrational and mistaken qualities, and worked on simply performing a task just as it is without the interfering thoughts, you are ready to recognize and develop the positive aspects of your situation that you may be missing—the other side of the yin-yang. This entails doing an open-focus meditation using gratitude, followed by a focus meditation using visualization in step four. Both of these meditations will help bring better balance to your thinking.

Exercise 9.3   Gratitude Meditation

You can direct your attention to take on a positive focus using this meditation. Sit quietly for a few moments. Then open your attention to list several things that you are grateful for in your life. You might think that you have nothing to feel thankful about, but once you start looking, you may be surprised to find that you have many things to feel grateful for. Your gratitude could come from such simple pleasures as eating a delicious cookie, seeing a beautiful bird fly by, or even sitting in the shade of a large tree on a warm, sunny day. You might feel grateful for certain people in your life, the education you have had, or a pet that you love. Let yourself be open to searching for these things and you will be surprised at how many you can find. Review your gratitude list regularly. Return to this meditation often, especially if you find your thoughts becoming negative.

Step Four: Allow

All the work that you have done begins a process of transformation. Step four allows the change process that you have set in motion to take hold. The effects of meditation occur over time. You have made some alterations in your thinking that ripple through your brain and nervous system, as we described in chapters 2 and 3, to help calm your limbic system and enhance the connections from your prefrontal cortex. You can facilitate the process by allowing these changes to grow.

Exercise 9.4   Focus on Allowing Change

You can focus your mind on gratitude to elicit a healing response within. This experience can become a resource for developing your positive qualities.

Sit quietly for a few moments and focus your attention on your breathing. Notice as each breath flows in and out, and allow your breathing to be natural. Now, vividly imagine that situation, person, or place you are grateful for. Notice how you might feel relaxed and happy in that circumstance. Vividly imagine yourself in this situation, feeling comfortable and at ease with yourself. Remain relaxed as you imagine it, picturing it and vividly recalling as many details as possible. Hold the idea, image, or feeling vividly in mind, and the natural ideomotor response will take place. Even small experiences can become a resource to help you handle your life better.

Do this meditation often, nonjudgmentally visualizing yourself having confidence, feeling good, even being inspired—simply being that confident person you can be at times. Response builds over time, so be patient with the process.

Raising Your Energy

You may start to feel a little better as you alter your thinking patterns. But your feelings of depression are also perpetuated by the lower activation of your nervous system. You can help to lift your mood by working on your energy level. Many problems, including depression, involve what Chinese medicine calls *stagnant chi* (Ming 2001). You can get your energy moving again by using some of the meditation methods you have already learned and adding some variations. These exercises focus attention on your body to activate your nervous system and allow your energy to flow freely for the pleasant effect of gently lifting your depressed mood.

Exercise 9.5 Focus on Freeing Your Stagnant Chi

This exercise builds on the skills of tightening and relaxing your muscles. The action of tightening and loosening can foster the free flow of chi for raising your energy.

Stand with your legs shoulder-width apart and your arms hanging loosely at your sides. Close your eyes. Make fists with your hands, and tighten your arm and hand muscles lightly. As you do this, focus all your attention on your arms and hands. Notice the sensations; feel the muscles contract. Keep all your concentration on this alone for approximately thirty seconds. Then, let your hands open, and relax your hands and arms. Notice how they feel; perhaps they feel longer when you release them. Pay attention to any sensations. Remain relaxed for about thirty seconds. Repeat this tightening and loosening five times, maintaining your mental focus throughout.

If you feel able to do so, try this exercise with your hands raised above your head, arms extended in front of you or out from your sides. Follow the same pattern of tension and relaxation, focusing your attention. Eventually you will begin to feel tingling or warmth in your hands. Inner energy is beginning to flow.

Exercise 9.6   Focus on Circulating Your Chi

Once you have successfully felt energy in your hands and arms, you can begin to experiment with circulating it. Do the previous exercise. When you feel warmth or tingling in your hands, imagine the tingling moving up your arms. Picture it moving into your shoulders. With time, you can direct it all around, especially to areas that need it for health and well-being. Circulate chi like fresh air. This exercise improves with practice and works best when you maintain your mental focus.

Exercise 9.7   Unblock Energy with Meditative Movement

Meditative movement is another way to free your energy. This is such a natural and easy activity that you can use it when you are feeling depressed or manic. Just adjust the pace, moving very slowly when you want to calm your energy, and moving a little more briskly when you want to raise your energy.

Meditative movement is most enjoyable when done in a beautiful setting in nature, such as in a park or the mountains or by water. But you can do it anywhere, even at home or in the office. We encourage you to do regular meditative movement when you are working to change a condition. Even a few minutes can set a process in motion.

Take off your shoes. Stand for a moment, relaxed and aligned with gravity. Very slowly, begin to move your arms forward and back, up and down, and around in a circle. Breathe comfortably and naturally, inhaling as you extend your arms out and exhaling as you retract your arms inward. Let your movements be slow, relaxed, and flowing. Allow your body to follow your arms, shifting your balance slightly from left to right and forward and back, and twisting your upper body gently. Don't force your movements. Keep them within a comfortable movement range. Pay careful attention to your sensations while you move. Continue to move and keep your attention on your sensations while breathing comfortably. Try slower or faster speeds of movement while staying meditatively aware.

When you feel ready to stop, stand quietly for several minutes. Sense your body now. You might feel tingling sensations, have a sense of energy circulating all around, and feel alert and refreshed. Enjoy this experience.

Energy Visualization Methods

Visualization methods can also help to regulate energy. Since the mind and body are linked through the ideomotor effect, you can use your own ability to visualize to stimulate your nervous system and raise your internal energy. These meditations combine focus and no-focus meditations. You begin by focusing your attention on a visualization, and then simply wait with open attention as you allow the effect to occur.

Exercise 9.8   Visualize Your Vital Force

Do this exercise while lying down with your legs and arms relaxed.

Close your eyes and form a mental picture of chi moving through your body. Imagine that it comes in through your nose as you inhale, and then moves down into your lungs. When you exhale, send all this energy to every part of your body, to your very fingertips and toes. Repeat for several minutes. Breathe naturally, without forcing or pushing your breath. Keep a vivid picture in your mind. Perhaps the energy is like light or water. Use an image that makes sense to you. Then wait and allow the effects to take place in your body.

When you are finished, open your eyes and stretch. You may feel tingling, warmth, or some sense of vitality.

Exercise 9.9 Focus on Visualizing a Healthy Balance

Sit or lie down, whichever is more comfortable.

Imagine that you are very healthy and balanced. Perhaps you can recall a specific time, before you ever had a bipolar episode, when you felt especially good. Or maybe you would like to create an image of your body as healthy. Visualize your chosen image as vividly as possible. Imagine how you would feel if you were balanced and had steady moods. Notice every detail. Sometimes people like to imagine that they are doing something and enjoying it. Or you might like to simply recall the sensations you have when you are in balance. Experiment to find what works for you.

Do this meditation daily while you are working on changing.

Conclusion

Keep working with each negative thought or feeling. First, become aware of it. Then question it. Next, imagine a more mature, realistic thought or feeling. And finally, allow a new experience to take place. Don't blame yourself for having negative thoughts or low energy. After all, during your bipolar episodes, certain nervous-system patterns occur, making it harder to do things. Practice the energy-raising exercises regularly and be patient. A change in your nervous system takes time, so have compassion for yourself and recognize the efforts you are making. Once you commit yourself to changing, you may find that your depression is not as intractable as you expected.

Chapter 10

Harmonize Your Mania

You probably like your manic phase. Many bipolar sufferers do. You feel confident, energetic, and full of great ideas when you are experiencing the early stage of the elevated phase of your cycle. But as your mood progresses, it inevitably becomes overly intense. You may engage in dangerous or foolish behaviors that you often regret later. And even though you have a great deal of energy, you are likely to find yourself easily irritated and short tempered. People who are close to you complain about what you are doing and may become angry with you, because it affects them too. So, even though you may like your manic phase, you know that there are problems associated with it.

You can learn how to moderate your manic moods and keep some of that positive energy without letting it carry you away. You can slow down your racing thoughts and yet remain alert and aware. Recall that meditation has the dual effects of enhancing both alertness and relaxation simultaneously (see chapter 3). By calming your nervous system meditatively when it is overaroused, you remain alert and energetic. You will be able to use your energy productively and direct it into meaningful endeavors.

This chapter provides meditation methods that help you direct your energy toward finding a healthy balance in your manic moods. The meditations in this chapter will help you realign your flow of energy to be in harmony with the rhythms of your body. Meditation methods for preventing impulsive behaviors are also provided. You can calm down when you become overly elated. In addition, you will learn how to take steps that can prevent a mood swing before it happens.

Meditating when you are feeling energetic and elated has certain challenges. Your thought processes are quicker, so you may find yourself easily distracted, or your associations may wander. As soon as you notice that your mind has moved away from the particular meditation, gently bring yourself back. Continuing to return to the meditation develops patience. You will begin to notice a gradual slowing down of your thoughts as you regain more stable attention.

Moderating Your Energy

Energy (chi) moves through your body all the time. When you are not having your bipolar symptoms, your energy levels correspond naturally to the day-night cycle. You usually feel alert and energetic during the day, and calm and quiet at night. But when you have a bipolar mood swing, your energy is not in harmony with the natural rhythms of the day-night cycle. The fluctuations in energy become extreme, causing you to be out of sync with your healthy rhythms.

Breathing Meditations for Balanced Alertness

The breath is the gateway to emotion, as we discussed in chapter 5. Breathing meditations have long been used as part of Taoist healing methods. A full, relaxed breath brings in fresh oxygen and expels stagnant chi from the body. In addition, breathing meditations have the dual effects of alerting and calming. As you notice each breath, your attention becomes less scattered and more focused, leading you to be alert and in touch. At the same time, your breathing steadies and becomes more natural, helping you to feel calm and centered in your experience.

You are likely to breathe differently when you are manic from how you breathe when you are feeling depressed. Do the following three breathing meditations at various times in your cycles and at different times of the day or evening. They will help you ease your overactivated nervous system, find a balanced level of energy, and then simply allow a calm, clear moment to enjoy it.

Exercise 10.1 Open Focus: Notice Your Breathing

Lie down comfortably on your back. Breathe mindfully through your nose for several minutes, carefully noticing your breathing just as it is, without judging. Do you perceive some tightness? Perhaps your breathing is heavy, or maybe your breaths are short. Simply observe for several minutes. In time you will get to know how you typically breathe when your mood is elevated, depressed, or somewhere in between.

Next, place your hands, palms down, lightly on your abdomen. Pay attention to your hands, noticing how they move up as you breathe in and down as you breathe out. Breathe comfortably, observing the rise and fall of your hands. Keep focused on your hands and the movement in your abdomen. In time, your breathing will settle into a relaxed, natural pattern. You might find that tension releases and your breathing becomes more relaxed and comfortable.

Exercise 10.2 Focus on Balancing the Breath

Now do this alternate-nostril breathing meditation to balance your energy between the two sides of your body while enhancing your concentration.

Curl the first two fingers of your right hand and rest your thumb against the curled fingers while pointing up. Extend your fourth and fifth fingers out straight. Cover your right nostril with your thumb and inhale through your left nostril, with a natural, relaxed breath. Then shift your hand to block your left nostril with the extended fingers, and exhale through your right nostril, doing a complete exhalation. Inhale and exhale comfortably through your right nostril, and then block it while inhaling, exhaling, and inhaling with the other nostril. Alternate back and forth in this way for five to ten breath cycles. Keep your breathing relaxed and comfortable.

Exercise 10.3   No Focus: Just Breathe

Now that you have found your balanced, natural breathing rhythm, sit quietly for several minutes, and simply allow yourself to breathe comfortably and enjoy the experience. Don't try to do anything to alter your breathing. Simply breathe as you do. Let your mind clear as you sit quietly. If a thought comes along, notice it, and then return to just breathing. Maintain this meditation until you feel like stopping. Return to it often, even if for only a few minutes, to simply let yourself be clear and open.

Becoming Mindful of Your Typical Tension Patterns

You can become meditatively aware of yourself at the body level, in order to get to know some typical tension patterns that accompany the phases of your cycle. If you release tension, your chi can flow as it should for a more comfortable, relaxed balance.

Do the next exercise at a time when you are feeling overstimulated.

Exercise 10.4   Body Scan for Tension

Lie down in a comfortable place. Scan your body and notice the general tone of your muscles. Then, beginning at your head, notice the muscles in your face. Are you holding any part tightly, such as your lips, forehead, or eyes, while other areas are relaxed? You may carry pockets of tension in a particular area, without ever noticing. Using your attention, carefully trace the pattern of tension. So, if you feel a pulling sensation between your eyes and forehead, notice each part of the pattern. Do you feel discomfort? Or perhaps you feel nothing, even numbness? Sometimes such patterns have a sense of familiarity, especially if you have carried this tension for a long time. Instead of dwelling on what the sensation means or any other thoughts about it, keep focused on the body sensations themselves. Notice everything about what you feel in your head: temperature or sensations. Don't change anything; simply notice.

Then move down to your neck and shoulders. Sense whether you find tightness in your neck and shoulders. You can find one clue to whether your neck and shoulders are tight by noticing how these areas meet the floor, bed, or couch you are lying on. If they are tight, you will probably feel that they are either lifted slightly away from the floor or bed, or pressing down hard. Once again, notice any accompanying sensations without changing anything. Continue down until you have attended to your entire body, just noticing tense areas and relaxed ones in this way. When you are finished, move on to the next exercise.

Exercise 10.5 Ease Tensions

Start again at your head by paying attention to your face. If you discovered tension in a particular area, such as your eyes, forehead, or lips, turn your attention there. First, carefully trace how you are holding these muscles, as you did in the last exercise, and then, if possible, allow these muscles to relax. Let go. These muscles will feel softer, lighter, larger, or smoother. Breathe comfortably and let the tension go with each exhalation of breath. Then direct your attention down toward your shoulders, paying close attention to them. Notice whether you are holding your muscles tightly, and let go if possible. If you notice that your shoulders are held away from the floor, can you let them sink down and accept support from the surface? Continue down through your body, first paying close attention and then relaxing any extra tension. You may be surprised to notice areas that are tightly tensed but don't need to be. If your attention wanders to outer concerns, bring it back. Don't force yourself to relax. Simply notice where you can or cannot relax, and gently keep trying to let go of unnecessary tension.

Prevention

When you are in your manic phase, you may lose awareness of what you are doing or saying at times. You probably aren't listening to your body's needs. You may miss feelings of hunger or tiredness. And when you are feeling depressed, you might ignore your body's needs because you are unable to make the effort. In both ends of the cycle, your attention is distracted. So, where is your attention directed? Mindfulness meditation can help you to find the answer, and then, once you know, you will be able to do something about it and return your attention to your body's built-in signals to sleep when you are tired and eat when you are hungry. Listen to your inner signals.

Enlisting Mindfulness to Attune to Your Cycles

Teresa was out of touch with what she was doing. As she began to move toward her highs, she stopped eating and sleeping but didn't really notice. She found that her attention was directed to the many projects she wanted to complete. When she wasn't busy cleaning or rearranging things at home, she was out partying with friends. But things always got out of hand. And when she was depressed, Teresa didn't feel like doing anything. She spent this time lying in bed or sitting alone at home. She missed so much work that she used up all of her vacation time. Even though Teresa took her medication, it wasn't working that well. She needed something more.

We taught Teresa to meditate. She practiced mindful awareness so that she could notice what she was doing as she did it. The only constant in her life was photography. She took hundreds of pictures when she was manic, but even when she felt depressed, she managed to make herself snap a few pictures. We encouraged her to begin her practice of mindfulness when she took pictures. She noticed the subtle qualities of light. She felt the weight of her camera as she held it steady. And she examined the patterns. She enjoyed being mindful so much, because it opened a new way of looking at the world. Her work took on a depth of feeling that made her pictures beautifully unique.

She felt motivated to be mindful in other situations. She extended her meditation to times when she wasn't taking pictures. As she did, she began to notice when she was skipping meals. She told us, "I feel like my whole body is humming. I have no appetite and feel a kind of ragged energy." She noticed that she was doing stimulating activities late into the night, which made her unable to sleep and uninterested in eating. With this awareness, she reflected on what she was doing and then made different choices. She deliberately sat down to eat three meals each day, and meditated to slow down at night so that she could get more sleep.

Exercise 10.6 Be Mindful of Your Energy during an Enjoyable Activity

Begin this mindfulness meditation when you are doing something that you enjoy, as Teresa did with photography. Pay close attention to the activity as you do it. Stop at times, if possible, to notice your body sensations, your emotions, and your thoughts. Use the skills you developed in chapter 6 to simply notice without judging things as good or bad. When you complete the activity, sit or stand quietly for a moment and notice your experiencing.

Exercise 10.7 Be Mindful of Your Energy during an Upswing

Now, practice mindfulness meditation when you sense yourself going into an upswing but aren't quite there yet. Notice your eating and sleeping patterns. Look at the charts you've been keeping since chapters 1 and 2. Do you observe the patterns of an upswing or downswing? Are you tempted to skip a meal? If so, stop and pay attention to your stomach. Do you feel hungry and ignore the signs? Perhaps you are trying to accomplish something and feel that you don't have time to eat. If so, sit quietly in meditation for a few minutes to center yourself in the present moment. Recognizing that skipping meals tends to lead to imbalances, allow yourself to take a few minutes to eat. Meditate again at your typical bedtime, even if you don't feel tired. Center yourself in the moment. Encourage yourself to quiet down and prepare for sleep. By noticing your daily routines, you might be able to intervene and prevent a cycle from happening.

Rediscovering Your Natural Rhythms

Mindful awareness of how you prevent yourself from sleeping and eating is one side of the yin-yang spectrum for intervening in your mood swings. But you can also invite your body to respond, as in exercise 7.5, "Wu Wei: Indirect Mind Clearing," and let nature take its course.

Living at one with the Tao involves recognizing your part in the greater universe. You are a part of nature, even though you might sometimes lose touch with that connection, especially if you live in an urban area. And yet, your world has its rhythms of daylight and darkness, and seasonal changes no matter where you live. Your brain has an internal clock, located in the hypothalamus, that regulates your body states. It's the seat of the biological clock, the circadian rhythms for sleep and waking. The hypothalamus is also involved in regulating your feelings of hunger and fullness. By connecting meditatively with your greater environment, you can help your body to align with the rhythms of nature and stop interrupting the natural ability of the hypothalamus to regulate your sleep-wake cycle and your eating schedule.

Meditation can allow your nervous system to return to its healthy, natural balance. The following series of meditations offers focus meditations using visual imagery. Recent research finds that people with bipolar disorder tend to rely more heavily on internal imagery than the general population does (Holmes et al. 2008), and that using mental imagery therapeutically can be especially helpful (Ball et al. 2006; Holmes and Mathews 2010). Practice the sun and moon visualization meditations and the hunger meditation regularly for several weeks, along with the previous two mindful-of-energy exercises. In time, your efforts will help you to make better choices that move you toward regular sleeping and eating patterns.

You can encourage your nervous system to return to its normal wake-sleep cycle by meditating. The traditional meditations below are intended to enhance vitality by day and calm your energy by night, in response to the sun and the moon. During these meditations, you may wish to recall memories of the sun and the moon, or perhaps create new images.

Exercise 10.8 Visualize the Sun's Light

Practice this meditation during daylight hours. You can do it outdoors or inside, perhaps near a window that allows light in. Sit quietly and breathe comfortably. Notice the light as it fills the area where you are sitting. Imagine that the sun shines down on you (or if you are sitting outside in the sun, feel the warm sunlight on your skin). Imagine that the light penetrates through you so that you feel aglow with the bright, warm light of the sun. Imagine that you soak in the energy, that the sun's rays stimulate your inner energy to flow freely and unobstructed. You might begin to feel some tingling sensations or warmth develop in your hands or feet. If so, let the feeling spread. Remain relaxed as you think about the sun.

Exercise 10.9 Visualize the Moon's Luminescence

Do this meditation in the evening, when it's dark outside. Sit quietly and breathe comfortably as before. This time, imagine a full moon above (or if you are sitting outside under the moon's glow, pay attention to the moon) and notice the gentle radiance of the moon's glow on your skin. Let the luminescence penetrate through you so that you feel yourself glowing with the soft, silvery light. Notice the sensations of calm from the soft light. Let your energy quiet down within as you remain relaxed, contemplating the moon's calming light.

Nurturing Balanced Hunger

You may not feel like eating when you are manic, and when you are depressed, you might find that you eat too much. Your body has a built-in system for regulating hunger, and during your normal phase, you probably have a regular eating schedule that includes three meals a day. But your bipolar symptoms mask these natural inner signals. Or you might simply disregard them. Cultivating awareness of your body's signals can help you to prevent your cycle from taking over.

Exercise 10.10   Focus on Hunger

Practice this focus meditation each time you typically have a meal. Sit quietly in your dining area and turn your attention to your body sensations. Notice any sensations in your stomach and thoughts that you might be having. Imagine the meal you might have. Think about its preparation and visualize yourself eating. Spend several minutes thinking about your meal and noticing your body sensations. You might begin to feel your natural hunger. If so, take the time to eat your meal. If not, eat a small amount of nourishing food anyway. Do this meditation at each mealtime. Eventually, your body's natural ability to know when you are hungry and recognize when you are full will reassert itself to guide you to healthy eating. And in doing so, you will have better balance in your energy.

Exercise 10.11   Eat Mindfully

When you sit down to eat, turn your attention to the act of eating. Don't talk. Instead, notice your process of experiencing. If you are eating with others, tell them about the exercise, and perhaps they will join you in mindful eating.

Look at the food, smell the aromas, see the colors, and notice the shapes and textures. As you begin, chew each bite gently all the way, tasting the food. After you swallow, pay attention to how the food feels in your stomach. Listen to your body's signals for the need to eat more or a sense of fullness. When you are finished, sit for a moment to notice your body's sensations.

Controlling Your Impulses

There are many factors involved in how you decide to do something. Sometimes you will look at your options and think carefully about what you want to do. You will carefully weigh out the risks and rewards, and balance out how much you expect to gain or lose over time. Your brain processes these kinds of decisions through a long path that involves your thinking brain, in the prefrontal cortex.

But when you are having an elevated mood, you are more likely to make your decisions impulsively, without giving them much thought. These kinds of decisions are processed in the brain through a short neural path that goes directly between your sensations and your emotional brain, bypassing your thinking processes entirely. This fast-acting system responds to physiological urges. Your body signals the urge, and based on these signals, you just do things impulsively.

There is a mediating process, known as *interoception*, that links the short path and the long path, and it is found in the right-anterior insula, an area tucked deep in the cortex between the frontal and temporal lobes. Interoception is your internal body sense, that gut feeling that you have when you know something feels right or wrong. In a sense, the insula guides you to either push the accelerator to drive an impulse or press the brakes to stop it. The core idea is that your internal body states are more involved in what you feel and do than you might think.

Research shows that when interoception malfunctions, you make risky or impulsive decisions. During your depressed moods, you probably appraise your interoceptive experiences more negatively (Paulus et al. 2003). Problems with interoception will affect your decision-making ability. You might act more impulsively with drugs, sex, or emotions, when you are in an elevated mood, because your decisions are more driven by short-path sensations than long-path thought.

There are several ways to use meditation to improve your interoception sense, thereby reducing your impulsiveness and improving your decision making: sharpening your awareness, refraining from judging what you notice, and shifting your reactions to the long path. The meditations in this section offer concrete ways to get better control over your impulsive behaviors.

Exercise 10.12   Open Focus: Sharpening Interoception Awareness

Meditation works directly with interoception, providing the sensitivities and clarity that you may be missing.

Scan through your body, noticing your sensations from head to toe, and then turn your attention to your muscles. Notice where your muscles are tight and where they are loose. Pay attention to your breathing. Notice the air that goes in through your nose, the sensation as it travels down through your breathing passages into your lungs and then out again as you exhale. Next, pay attention to your body temperature. Does your skin feel warm or cool? You may notice variations, such as warmth in your midsection or face, and coolness in your hands or feet. Now, turn your attention to your heartbeat. Is your heart beating hard, or can you barely feel it? Place your hand lightly on your chest at your heart if you are having difficulty feeling it. Move your attention deeper within. Do you feel any sensations in your stomach or chest? You might feel pulsing somewhere or maybe internal heat or coolness. Let your attention be directed to the inside of your body, and notice any sensations you might be having. Take a mindful glance to your inner experiencing often. In time, you will sharpen your inner sensing.

Exercise 10.13 Interoception without Judgment

You may tend to assess your sensing as overly negative when you are feeling depressed. Here is an opportunity to set aside your criticisms and practice nonjudgmental awareness. Begin by noticing that you are judging. So, if you tended to observe pain and discomfort when you did the previous exercise, start again, only this time dig below the surface label "painful" and describe the deeper pain sensation more specifically. Is it hot, cold, sharp, or dull? The sensation may be intense or barely perceptible. Search for more descriptive words. If you make a judgment, be aware *that* you are judging; for example, *Now I am judging this sharp sensation as painful.* Separate the judgment (*good, bad, awful, wonderful, terrible*) from the pure sensation. Notice and accept each sensation as just what it is.

Stop-for-a-Minute Meditations

The awareness you are developing can be a resource to help you gain control over your impulses. But sometimes, as we discussed earlier, your impulses happen fast, often without much thinking. You can intervene with your impulses by shifting your reactions from the short path to the long path. And you can do so quickly by adding a one-minute meditation. Next time you feel an impulse to do something, stop and set the timer on your watch for one minute. Then, do one of these one-minute meditations.

Exercise 10.14 One-Minute Focus on One Thing

Pick one inner sensation to focus on. Keep your attention focused on this one sensation for the entire minute. If your attention drifts, stop meditating and rest for a second or two. Then, bring your attention back to the sensation and return to your meditation until the minute is over.

Exercise 10.15 Open Focus: Minute Mindfulness

Turn your attention inward and open your focus to whatever you are experiencing now. Allow your attention to flow wherever it goes. Notice experiencing as it is, without judging it as good or bad. And ground your awareness in the present moment by affirming, *Now I am aware of thinking of yesterday*, or *Now I am thinking of what I will do later*. Stay with the present as it changes in each moment.

Exercise 10.16 No Focus: Minute Mind Clearing

Sit or stand, and let your mind clear of all thoughts. You may want to imagine an empty space, such as a clear lake or a single color. Or just allow your thoughts to settle and slow until your mind clears.

Exercise 10.17 Bring It All Together: One-Minute Centering

Take a moment to center yourself in your environment by experiencing your surroundings, looking around, noticing your feet on the ground, feeling the temperature of the room, and so on. Then, notice what you are experiencing within. And finally, allow yourself to just be where you are now, centered in the moment, calm and steady.

Practicing these one-minute meditations often makes them easier to do, plus it helps you turn to them more readily when you need them. All of the meditations in this section will help you to shift from automatic, reflexive reactions toward more-thoughtful, aware responses.

Balancing Impulsiveness with Spontaneity

Spontaneity is one of the key elements in living life in tune with the Tao. Spontaneity is healthy. According to Dr. Adolph Meyer, the founder of psychobiology and a major leading figure in early psychotherapy in the United States, the mark of mental health is spontaneity. He said, "It is spontaneity that I want to study and inquire into, and cultivate and respect as the all-important quality of a person" (Meyer 1948, 581).

Spontaneity arises from within the deeper, emerging parts of your nature. Developing your spontaneity allows you to express and evolve your potential.

But as a bipolar sufferer, you know that simply following a spontaneous impulse doesn't always lead you in good directions. This happens when your impulse is out of touch with the Tao in the larger context of your life, which includes others in your life.

Spontaneous responses that keep you in tune with your true nature are in balance with your whole being, including your situation, your own needs and reactions, and the needs of those you care about. Like water, the formless Tao takes on the form of the cup you pour it into.

So true spontaneity never loses sight of balance between yin and yang. "Spontaneous" doesn't have to mean losing connection to anything tangible or reasonable. Allow spontaneous impulses to emerge in response to circumstances without losing the center of life, the Tao. In this way, you can flow with impulses, inner feelings, needs, and reactions while not getting swept away by them. When you are in tune with the Tao, you know when to begin and when to end.

Exercise 10.18   Open Focus: Impulse

Spontaneity evolves from an unplanned impulse, but its usefulness requires restraint. Having experienced the pull of impulse that can lead you away from balance, you will benefit from learning how to sit quietly and close your eyes. Let yourself relax for a few minutes and do nothing. Eventually, an impulse to do or think something will arise within. Let it emerge, and try to be aware of it as it arises. But don't do anything about it: simply observe mindfully that you are having an impulse to do something.

Exercise 10.19   No Focus for Spontaneity: At One with the Tao

The Taoist idea of spontaneity is to remain in tune with the Tao. Then your spontaneous desire will always be the best one, taking you in a productive, positive direction rather than leading you into a high or a low. This exercise is designed to attune you to the larger perspective. Keep the whole in mind, so that you don't lose sight of the Tao of your whole being and all you are meant to do in your life to fulfill your destiny.

Clear your mind and relax quietly. Wait for an impulse to emerge, but remain aware of the broader context. For example, if your desire is to relax by reading a book but you have to be at work in an hour, keep the greater whole in mind. Usually your impulse alters naturally to reflect the greater Tao. When you attune your spontaneous impulse to the larger Tao of your life situation, you can sense whether you want to read and then go to work, or whether you can stay home and unwind, without interfering with your job or your own needs.

Practice these two meditations often when you are struggling with impulses. Gradually you will find your impulses becoming more aligned with your greater needs, leading you toward actions and decisions that are more in tune with what is healthy and helpful for you.

Conclusion

You can learn to harness your energy deliberately so that you can use it to accomplish what you want to do in life. With awareness and the willingness to meditate, you can realign your reactions with your natural body rhythms and find a healthy harmony. And by enhancing your inner awareness, you will gain control over your impulses; calm yourself when you are overactivated; and stay centered, alert, and aware in the moment.

Chapter 11

Balance Your Relationships

Your moods strongly influence your relationships. You probably interact very differently when you are on an upswing from when you are feeling down. Extreme differences in how you relate make it difficult for your loved ones to know how to respond. And you may have contradictory feelings about them as well. With all the inconsistencies, misunderstandings can arise, putting a strain on your interpersonal relationships.

This chapter provides meditations for improving your relationships. Since your reactions tend to differ depending on your mood, we provide methods for when you are in your upswing and when you are feeling down. Of course, both moods are still sides of you. You strengthen your continuity in relating as you find more balance in your life. Your deeper nature shines through consistently to enhance the quality and satisfaction of your relationships.

Are you sometimes immersed in your projects and other people, and then, other times, withdrawn from people and activities? Perhaps you are surprised to learn that people are annoyed or just disappointed with you. This is because you are likely to function between two relationship extremes—other-centered to self-centered—depending on your mood. The next two sections help you to find a more balanced way to interact even when you are experiencing strong moods.

Enhancing Your Relationships When You Are Manic

During an upswing in mood, you may want to participate in various social events: parties, outings, group dinners, and celebrations. The drive and energy to engage in such events is perpetuated during the up part of your cycle. You may find yourself wanting to help others, which is a positive impulse. But sometimes you may be generous to an unwise extreme, giving away money or other benefits, and even forcing them on others when they may not actually wish for or merit them. You need to moderate your social, generous tendencies so that your best qualities work well for you and others. During extreme moods, it's hard to judge correctly, but when you moderate these tendencies, you open the way for better judgment and improved relationships.

Nurturing Balanced Benevolence

Sara was on an upswing. She loved her friends and enjoyed lavishing them with gifts. She spent time at the mall buying designer purses and clothes for her best friends, items she couldn't afford. Her generosity impulse was strong, and even though she tried, she couldn't stop herself from acting on it. We advised her, rather than continue to fail in her attempts to stop it, to accept her generosity meditatively. We also taught her some of the mindful meditations in this chapter for listening to others.

During one session, we proposed a therapeutic outing to a clothing store that sold moderately priced items. As she shopped for her friends, we suggested that she maintain focused attention while shopping. She realized that she enjoyed the experience of looking for nice things for those she cared about. She could see that the price tag wasn't what fulfilled her. What she really liked was expressing generosity itself, being generous. She found some beautiful things to buy and left the store having spent under a hundred dollars! Later, when she was no longer in her cycle, her friends shared with her that the extravagant gifts had made them more uncomfortable than happy. Gradually she learned that by accepting her impulse to be generous, she could moderate it in a way that was appropriate for her finances and for others.

Exercise 11.1   Moderation

Practice this meditation to learn about the basis of being overly generous. First, sit quietly for a few minutes and pay attention to the present moment. Then turn your attention inward and recall a generous act that you did once, even if it was a small one. In your imagination, try to vividly experience the situation with your senses. Now search deeper. Can you find the generous impulse underlying your wish to perform the action? Accept the prior impulse of generosity and stay with it for a few minutes, noticing the sensations, thoughts, and meanings that go with it or the excitement and happiness associated with it. Attune to the feeling of generosity and seek the implicit benevolence there. Accept these qualities, just as they are. Accept yourself. As you do, allow your body to relax and a feeling of calm to develop.

The old saying "It's the thought that counts" may apply here. Your generous thought does matter, and so does the intended recipient. A moderate expression of generosity may be more appreciated than an extreme one, and you will feel more enjoyment from including the other person in what you do.

Easing Your Irritable Interactions

You may become agitated, annoyed, or impatient with others. The excess energy of your upswing can bring irritability along with it. But elevated expression of these tendencies may lead to an extremely stressed state for you and your relationships (review chapter 8 for stress reduction).

For every yin, there is some yang. You can appreciate the complete fullness of the Tao by knowing both yin and yang. Similarly with your emotions, each polar opposite reveals an aspect of the greater whole, and in this sense, it is a source of information, a way of attuning to the world.

Anger, sadness, and frustration are feelings that you probably don't want to feel, and understandably so, but your problems with irritability arise when you are dissociated from what you feel. In the attempt to avoid discomfort, you lose a valuable tool that attunes you to your interactions. Your emotions, even the uncomfortable ones, are meaningful signposts when you accept and feel them through. The prickly cactus produces some of the world's most beautiful flowers. Learning to tolerate and embrace the range of your emotions can bring greater control.

Exercise 11.2   Mindful Attention to Your Irritability

The Tao of change begins when you, first, move closer to what you want to change. So, when you are feeling slightly frustrated, annoyed, or unhappy—but before you reach the point of taking it out on someone else—pause for a few moments of meditative focus to become aware. Sense your irritable feeling in the moment. Remember not to evaluate it, but simply notice what's there. If describing it is helpful, do so in terms of your own feeling, not in terms of what you imagine the other person is thinking, feeling, or doing. Notice any accompanying sensations in your body, such as tension in your stomach, neck, or back. Become aware of what thoughts are going through your mind, observe them as they occur, and accept them as they are. Allow the feeling and simply notice whatever is there, without thinking beyond it. Gradually the feeling will begin to alter, opening a window to your deeper emotional being in that moment. Stay with the feeling and perception, watching how it alters somewhat with each new moment.

Inviting Calm

Meditation brings calm. Sometimes irritable moods come from over-arousal of your nervous system. Take a few minutes each day to practice quiet sitting. Let your breathing be soft, like that of an infant, and allow your thoughts to slow. Use the stress-reduction exercise 8.6, "Find Your

Sanctuary," and relaxation exercises 10.3 through 10.5: "No Focus: Just Breathe," "Body Scan for Tension," and "Ease Tensions." As your feelings of irritability ease, you will find it easier to treat others with consideration and kindness.

Enhancing Your Relationships When You Are Depressed

During the down part of the cycle, your tendencies are different. This is just another side of you, yet it is still the same you, perhaps with a somewhat exaggerated intensity. During this time, you may feel tired and want to withdraw from others. You might worry about money or that you have spent too much of it. You might feel bored, sluggish, or irritable, not at your best, so to speak.

People rarely appreciate this part of the cycle, and often consider it a low point. And it is a low point. But great value is hidden in these moments, where you can regroup and recoup yourself. These lows can be opportunities for deeper relating.

Exercise 11.3 Turn Your Attention Outward

Sometimes, when you feel hopeless, gloomy, and despairing, the inward focus of your attention on yourself is not helpful. A shift in attentional focus can get you in touch with the flow of positive chi in your actual, outer circumstances with others, or your life situation, which is forming anew beyond your inner ruminations. You can deliberately turn your attention outward by focusing on an outer object.

Pick something beautiful in the room or perhaps outdoors. Focus your attention fully on it. Notice all the details. Then, close your eyes and picture it. If you forgot something, open your eyes again to look, and then close your eyes again. Continue to focus until you have a clear picture of the object in mind. Return to this meditation when you feel stuck.

Exercise 11.4 Suspend Judgment of Others

One of the keys to changing your mood is to keep attunement as your center of focus, not just your opinions or concepts of others or yourself. As discussed in earlier chapters, avoid judging others, and try to avoid judging yourself.

Turn your attention to someone you care about toward whom you perhaps have negative feelings. Apply the four-step method from chapter 9 to how you are thinking about this person. Begin by observing, and then question, imagine, and allow. Instead of criticizing yourself, you might be criticizing or blaming the other person. Go through all four steps to notice how you might be thinking about your loved ones in ways that lead to some of your discomfort with them. Gradually you will be better able to sort out what you or they might need to change.

Using Meditation to Forgive with Compassion

When you are depressed, you may feel annoyed and resentful of others. But holding on to resentments not only hurts your relationships; it also hurts you. The wise English author Samuel Johnson (1709 to 1784) provided timeless wisdom when he said, "A wise man will make haste to forgive, because he knows the true value of time and will not suffer it to pass away in unnecessary pain. Resentment is a union of sorrow with malignity, a combination of a passion which all endeavor to avoid with a passion which all concur to detest" (1966, 135).

Meditation can help you to cultivate forgiveness, even of those who may have wronged you. Learning not to take offense, to have compassion for the plight of others, and even to take some transgressions lightly will give you greater peace of mind. Your reactions will change, and you may even help others around you.

An open-focus meditation on compassion can help you to forgive. Meditate on how the person you resent might be suffering. This person's irritating interactions may be an expression of discomfort she feels within. You can imagine the pain this person may be experiencing. You might even know something about what this person has suffered in life. Because you understand what it feels like to suffer, you can feel compassion for someone else's suffering. You can use the depth of insight you have gained from your moods to recognize that others might suffer too, so that your pain serves as your teacher to help others.

Fostering Awareness of Others

Research has shown that people with bipolar disorder have difficulty recognizing emotions in the facial expressions of others. One study showed that bipolar I sufferers had significantly lower emotional recognition than people with bipolar II and normal subjects (Derntl et al. 2009). Another study found the same impaired perception of facial emotions in manic subjects. Depressed subjects had difficulty recognizing fear and disgust, but were able to accurately recognize the other emotions (Lembke and Ketter 2002). These deficits relate to the changes in the brain that occur with bipolar disorder. As a result, you may misperceive how others are feeling, including their feelings toward you. Misunderstandings may arise that complicate your interpersonal relationships. So don't jump to conclusions about the emotional states of others. Take time and make the effort to accurately empathize while incorporating feedback from the other person. We encourage you to train yourself to discern emotions better through meditation.

Exercise 11.5 Focus on Your Emotional Facial Expressions

Meditative awareness can help you to improve your accuracy in recognizing the emotions of others. Begin by looking at your face in a mirror. Now, think of something that makes you feel happy, and smile as you look at yourself in the mirror. Study your expression. Recognize your happy expression. Notice the details in your mouth, eyes, and eyebrows, as well as your face as a whole. Next, think of something that you feel sad about, and make a sad expression. Focus all your attention on your sad expression, noticing your mouth, eyes, and eyebrows, as well as your face as a whole. Now, think of something that makes you feel angry, and make an angry face. Study your face in the mirror and notice all the details you can about this expression. Next, think of something that makes you feel fearful. Look at your frightened face in the mirror and focus your attention on every detail. Finally, calm yourself in meditation for a moment and then study your facial expression.

Exercise 11.6   Focus on Others' Facial Expressions

Ask a friend or family member to help you with this exercise. Have this person think about each of the same emotions that you did in the previous exercise. Focus your attention on the other person's face and notice all the details. Then, guess what emotion you think is being expressed. If you have guessed correctly, focus again, thinking about the emotion being expressed while you look. Go through the four primary emotions: happiness, sadness, anger, and fear.

If possible, do this exercise with several different people. By carefully focusing your attention and receiving feedback about whether or not you are correct, you will improve your ability to recognize emotions in others.

Exercise 11.7   Focus on Listening

You are accustomed to thinking about the meaning of people's words, but you may rarely pay attention to the sound of a person's voice. Voice tones express emotions, just as do facial expressions. You can enhance your skills by turning your attention to the sound of the voice.

Focus your attention on your voice tones as you speak. Then, focus your attention on a friend's voice tones in conversation. Extend this meditation by listening when a loved one speaks while the person is feeling each of the primary emotions. Listen to others as they speak to you in many different situations. You may be surprised by how much information is conveyed in the tone of the voice, not just the words.

You can also turn your focus on the larger context of the situation, to grasp the emotional significance. Use all your faculties, not just the ones you use for a quick assessment.

Exercise 11.8 Focus on Another Person's Breathing

Another way to attune to others is to observe their breathing patterns. Since emotion and breathing are linked, people's emotions are expressed by the quality of their breath. You can sense a change of emotion by watching for an alteration in breathing. You may typically overlook subtle cues from others, but now that you have practiced attending to your own breathing in meditation, you may find it easy to perceive the breathing of those you care about, and thereby understand them better.

Ask a loved one to join you for a moment in a meditative exercise. Sit quietly together and observe the other person's breathing. Notice the breathing rhythm. Try breathing in the same pattern. Breathing together can put you in touch with what the other person is feeling, resulting in greater empathy.

Working Things Through

Observe and take notes, or create a voice memo about what you feel and any resistance you may have to the awareness exercises in this section. You can learn from your own reactions as you begin to pay more attention to other people's feelings. Some of your relationship problems may lessen or even disappear as you become more aware and then consider how to reduce unnecessary conflict.

You may find that you have issues to deal with. Perhaps you have annoyances and unresolved misunderstandings that you have not addressed. Talking to your loved ones about your feelings, while also recognizing and listening to their feelings, can lead to resolution of misunderstandings that have gone unnoticed. The working-through process takes time, so be patient. If there are strong disagreements that you can't work out reasonably together, consider seeking a counselor or family therapist to help. When you work on relationships, it can be helpful to receive guidance from an objective professional.

Bringing Balance to Your Relationships

Learn to cultivate the yin aspect of relating when you are too yang, and to cultivate yang when you are too yin. Seek the balance. Keep in mind that when a dark mood comes on as you interact with someone you care about, there is a point of light within it. Sometimes, while in the midst of conflict, the deeper caring in your relationship is difficult to grasp. The pattern is not conceptual; it is an experience. Return to the Tao's wordless experience, the source, before you begin the process of conceptualizing.

Exercise 11.9   The Power of Just Looking

Eyes, when used to see deeply without thinking, point to the inner being, before all of the problems began. When you find that you just can't communicate with a loved one in words, stop and look directly into each other's eyes. Do so for several minutes. Breathe calmly as you sit and just look. You will find that the deeper caring shines through. We have often asked arguing couples to just look. They find that the conflict melts away as love shines through.

The source of something is found in the beginning, not the end. Search for the source of calm before the interpersonal problem takes place: as the problem is forming, not after. Even in the midst of the storm, there is a calm space, the eye of the hurricane. Go there when it begins, to the center, where the balance point is. Steadfast there, you escape the storm's fury. From this vantage point, you can use your energy well.

Exercise 11.10 Open Focus: Find Balance Using Mindfulness Briefly

If you notice that a mood is beginning to sweep over you when you are with someone you care about, sit down for a moment to meditate. Do a one-minute mindfulness meditation to become aware of what you are experiencing right in that moment. Encourage the other person to do so as well. Explain how to sit quietly and notice what you are experiencing without judging it or conceptualizing about it. Simply notice feelings, thoughts, and body sensations. Pay attention to your surroundings and anything else that is occurring right now. Don't put the experience into words. After a few minutes, resume the discussion. Perhaps you will find some mutual understanding now that you have shared a quiet moment together. Or, at least, you may be able to tap into your own calm center, which can help you to keep your mood balanced even when others can't be calm.

Shared Mindfulness

Learning to accept input from your significant other, your family, your doctor, and your therapist can widen the circle of your self-awareness. Incorporate their contributions to your sense of what's going on. Their input can help you stay on track so that you can express yourself as the positive, generous, and energetic person you are when you are at your best. Listening requires understanding.

Matt was unaware of his mood swings and typically ignored input from others. But now he was newly married and loved his bride very much. She joined him in his therapy sessions at times, and we taught them both how to meditate. They practiced regular and shared mindfulness meditations after dinner. As they enjoyed the closeness they felt from meditating together, Matt began to trust more of his wife's feedback concerning his moods. He learned to listen to her observations, knowing that they were nonjudgmental and objective. She told him when she saw that his mood was changing—and he listened! With two people aware of his mood swings, he found himself much better able to take the preventive measures described in chapter 10. He also was better able to moderate his emotions as they swept over him, which helped him to find balance. He was more open to his wife's needs, and their relationship deepened.

Exercise 11.11 Regular, Shared Mindfulness Meditation

Schedule a regular time each day to sit with your significant other for mindfulness meditation. Sense each other's presence, perhaps listening to the sound of your partner's breathing and your own, or looking at the other person while you are both sitting in meditation. Pay attention to the temperature of the room, the quality of the light, and the feeling of the air as it touches your skin. Scan through your inner experiencing as well, noticing your thoughts, feelings, and body sensations. Practice together for ten to fifteen minutes, or longer as you build stamina.

Using Feedback from Mindful Observations with a Trusted Friend

Feedback will help you get and stay on track, if you listen and let yourself learn from it. The insight you gain from the feedback can feed forward to help guide your actions. But feedback is most useful when it is just factual, not accompanied by judgment. Observe your own behavior, and then write it down; it's even better to describe it to your significant other, or someone you trust and care for. This works best with loved ones who will listen sympathetically, but at least they need to do their best to be as objective as you are. Then ask whether the other person sees the same meaning as you do in what you are doing.

Conclusion

You can enhance understanding and build trust using meditation. So take heart, trust those who care for you, and be patient with your situation and with your relationships. Your loved ones want to help, and together, you can find a positive way to cope well and adapt.

Your problems from bipolar disorder lessen when you have people close to you who provide helpful input, support, and corrective feedback. Ensure that they are trustworthy and willing to listen objectively. Then with your own awareness and their helpful input, you can stay on track, grounded in your actual circumstances. Your circle of mindfulness grows to include those you care about in shared mindfulness. Together, in the meditative moment, your relationships deepen, your problems dissolve, and you find meaning and fulfillment in your interactions with others.

Chapter 12

Nurture Your Potential

Much of this book has been devoted to dealing with your problems stemming from bipolar disorder. But you also have positive qualities that you can develop to help you find a balanced, happy life.

Bipolar disorder has been correlated with being more creative than the rest of the population (Murray and Johnson 2010). Statistics show that 10 percent of people who are in creative professions are bipolar (Goodwin and Jamison 2007). Recall that about 4.5 percent of the general population is diagnosed with bipolar disorder (Merikangas et al. 2007), so clearly, if you have this diagnosis, you are more likely to be a creative person.

Another unique quality is your capacity, at times, to be perceptive, mentally sharp, and highly motivated, especially when you are hypomanic. In such moments, you express your creative talents. Your mood swings can make things harder, but you can actualize your talents by undergoing certain life changes.

This chapter shows you how to create attunement with your Tao, to find and maintain the best path for fostering your creative potential. You will learn how to form a stable path, develop your talents, and live fully and meaningfully in every moment. Like steering a boat through turbulent winds and currents, you will find the optimal course for you.

Living according to the Tao involves creating a path to a fulfilling and meaningful life. One of the most helpful changes to make for stabilizing your bipolar mood swings is to establish lifestyle regularity (Colom and Lam 2005). You can arrange the circumstances of your life in practical ways to lessen the power of your moods. And as you follow your Tao, you develop enduring stability and balance that fits your creative nature.

You find the formless Tao always expressed in some form of yin and yang. You can best express your unformed creative nature through the form of your stabilized life, your path of daily routines. Returning to the form, like the cup that provides a vessel to hold formless water, you give yourself the structure you need to express your talents.

Henry was in his sixties when he discovered the value of stability for creating. He had suffered from bipolar disorder since his early twenties, passing through countless episodes of highs and lows. During his ups, he was a dynamo who could make things happen. He was an interior designer, and the homes he designed were spectacular. His work brought him invitations to exciting parties from grateful clients. But his bipolar swings always led him to party and drink too much. He became irritable, demanding, and unproductive. His wife felt angry and helpless. Eventually, things fell apart until he was hospitalized. Typically, the aftermath of the problems he created for himself while he was high would send him into a deep depression filled with regrets and despair.

When we saw him, he had lived through many of these cycles. He wanted to be able to express his talent with design but felt unable to do so, fearing another manic episode. He told us that whenever he worked, things got chaotic. Since every job and customer was unique, his schedule had to change to fit these different needs. He saw no other solution for controlling his moods than giving up his work. But Henry was unhappy. Life seemed drab and mundane, with no meaning. We talked with him about forging his Tao, a stable path that could foster his talents without causing him to lose his balance. He was intrigued.

Henry learned how to meditate. He did exercise 4.2, "Find Your Standing Posture," from chapter 4, and the three forms of meditation in part 2: focus, open focus, and no focus. He began to sense what he was doing moment by moment. He learned to calm his stress and question his negative thinking patterns. He also practiced meditations to balance his upswings.

His wife owned a small antiques store, which had been a lifelong dream of hers, now that she was retired from teaching. Henry had largely ignored her endeavors, because he had been too caught up in his own moods. But now he began to perceive an overlap between his work and hers. Perhaps they could bring their two passions together!

We encouraged him to create healthy routines as a firm foundation for his life. He had always been an early riser, so he instituted thirty minutes of meditation before breakfast. He and his wife decided that he would open her shop in the morning. He could consult with his clients at the shop, which was a perfect setting for a design meeting. His customers liked the antiques they saw, so he began to include some of her beautiful pieces in his interior designs. His wife would join him for lunch at the shop with food she brought. Then, he would leave to work on his designs and take care of any site visits he needed to do in the afternoon.

He also added exercise: a meditative walk before dinner along the tree-shaded streets near where they lived. Sometimes his wife would join him on these enjoyable walks. In the evenings, he and his wife sometimes had social time for dinner with friends or clients. But more often, they found pleasure in a quiet evening at home together, rediscovering the relationship they had been neglecting. Now that they were sharing their work, they found much to talk about. He felt less interest in attending flashy parties and more meaning in delving deeper into the life he was creating. He looked forward to his daily routines and found an anchor there.

So, no matter what pushes and pulls he felt, he stayed on his path. His designs evolved now that he was putting his heart and mind fully into his work and less on surface glamour. Most important, he felt that his life had meaning and that he was fulfilling his talents.

Forming Your Tao

Review the exercises in the "Prevention" section of chapter 10 to find healthy eating and sleeping routines. It's always essential to maintain a regular pattern of these basic needs that fits your nature. But here are some additional things you can do to create a stable and reliable path. Use the chart in chapter 2 to keep track of how you are doing.

- Find some time each day for meditation. Some people like to do it in the morning, while others find that late at night works better for them. Or perhaps you would prefer taking one or more short breaks during your day to get in tune using meditation.

- Schedule daily exercise. There is now strong scientific evidence that making exercise a regular part of your routine will improve your health outcomes when you have bipolar disorder (Goodrich and Kilbourne 2010). These researchers state that bipolar disorder is a quintessential mind-body problem, so it makes sense to incorporate exercise into treatment.

Playing a sport you enjoy may make it easier for you to keep working out. But if you are not athletic, do something as simple as walking, lifting very light weights, or participating in a regular class at the local gym. People often make the mistake of doing too much too soon, and then feel unable to maintain it. If you do no exercise, adding ten minutes a day may be a good place to start. Build from where you are without making unrealistic demands on yourself. In time, your body will thank you. You will find yourself naturally feeling motivated to do more.

- Schedule time to pursue something meaningful. If your work is your passion, be sure to give yourself time each day to do your work mindfully. Pay close attention to what you are doing as you do it. If your hobby is your deeper interest, make sure that you can devote some time each day to that. People often neglect to do the things they love, thinking there isn't time. But fulfilling your Tao means including those things that you have a natural inclination to pursue. You will find that the emotional satisfaction from these pursuits ripples through your life.

- Be mindful of the others in your life and look for meaningful overlaps. You may be overlooking the things you enjoy doing with your loved ones. Spend some shared time with those you care about, even if it's as simple as eating a meal regularly together or consistently making time for intimacy with your partner.

- Plan time for fun on a regular basis. Work is important, but a day of rest and relaxation is also essential for keeping balance. We have advised families to plan regular "family fun," a time for a shared outing: a trip to a museum, a movie, a park; or even for playing a game at home. Family fun doesn't have to be extravagant; it can be something local and accessible that you and those close to you will enjoy together.

Creating a routine that fits your needs and talents is essential. By maintaining regular meals, sleep, and exercise, and by setting aside time for meaningful work and enjoyment, you will bring reliability and balance to your life.

The starting point, the center, is your meditative experience. As you find your unique individual balance, you become able to shape your life. When you are willing to consider alternatives to how you have lived in the past, a new path forms. Learn to sense what is needed, and permit it. Pay attention to the various details of your life, and take them seriously as they emerge.

Listening Mindfully to the Call of Your Lifestyle

Creating the lifestyle that will work for you involves attuning to your Tao. Take a mindful glance for one or two minutes at various times throughout your day. Practice open-focus mindfulness, noticing what you are experiencing at key times. Sense what you need. So, perhaps as you pay attention, you notice that you are feeling exhausted and overworked in the afternoon. Did you push yourself too hard all morning? Perhaps you need to add a fifteen-minute relaxation meditation into your afternoon schedule. Or maybe you perceive that you feel bored. You may not have included any time for meaningful work or creative efforts. Be attuned to what you need and want for your life, and be sure to make it part of your lifestyle.

The Tao can guide you to what is fulfilling. You are inclined toward becoming complete; there is a tendency to seek balance and harmony: your homeostasis, which will begin to guide you subtly if you listen.

Developing Your Talents

Developing your talents leads you toward your deeper nature, your Tao. When you foster your talent, you are tapping into the flowing spirit of Tao. You have probably had moments in your life when you did something exceptionally well. Without you thinking about it, it just happened.

169

When you follow the Tao, you can perform with skill. At that moment, you are attuned to the deeper essence. Unfortunately, these moments of perfect skill may not happen very often, perhaps because you get in your own way. You can learn to change this.

The great Taoist sage Chuang Tzu discussed a dart-throwing contest where people were betting on the winner. When the stakes were small, everyone threw with skill. When stakes went higher, participants worried about their aim. When betting was for real gold, players became nervous and skill levels dropped. In all three cases, the players' abilities remained the same, but because one prize meant more than another, people let these external conditions weigh on their minds, which interfered with their performance. "He who looks too hard at the outside gets clumsy on the inside" (Chuang Tzu 1968, 201).

Exercise 12.1   Focus on Perfecting a Skill

When you are learning to improve a skill, mind is a key component. Bringing your mind and body together will speed your learning. Attention is a key component in learning, so doing focus meditations as you are developing your skill will help you perform even better.

Bring your attention to your breathing for several minutes. Then, focus on performing your skill as you do it. So, for example, if you are throwing darts, as in Chuang Tzu's example, keep your attention on the movements as you do them, not the prize. Let your thoughts stay directed on the process of picking up the dart, moving your arm, and throwing toward the target. If your thoughts drift away, stop, wait until your attention is redirected to your action, and then start again. Perform with focus, with your body, breathing, and mind unified in the activity itself. Repeat this process throughout your practice session. When you are finished, focus on breathing once again, as you allow the learning to be consolidated.

Exercise 12.2 No Focus: Performing a Skill

Now perform your skill again. This time, clear your mind and don't think about anything. Sit for several minutes and quiet your mind with meditation. When you feel ready, begin the activity. To continue the dart example, keep your mind clear as you allow your body to flow through the movements you know and have practiced so well. Don't fill your thoughts with the bull's-eye or points. Just let the dart fly from your hand. Your natural ability to hit the mark will be free to express itself without any mental doubts or worries to interfere.

Use meditation to develop many of your skills and talents. You will enhance your performance in all that you do. Stay aware of the process as you do it, and you will find deeper satisfaction and enjoyment in the doing itself.

Living Your Tao Fully and Meaningfully

However simple or complex your life is, it is all part of the Tao. But to express this, you must let yourself do it. Allow yourself to fulfill your meaningful roles in life and express your talents. So, if you are a parent or a spouse, don't interfere with yourself. Play your role fully. If you are a student, open yourself to learning. Do not fight it; flow with it. You participate in the Tao. You can be in school, work at a job, live as part of a family, and be in each facet of your life wholeheartedly. Let school, job, and family improve you, allowing you to grow.

Sages know how to participate in the Tao. They take an attitude that allows them to spontaneously follow the path they are on and be facilitated by the natural forces that are inevitably present. You, too, can receive what the world gives, and as you receive, you also give. Keep the balance. And you will find happiness and fulfillment, living in harmony with the natural flow of your life and abilities, expressed as oneness with the Tao.

Exercise 12.3 No Focus: The Tao

Sit quietly and allow your breathing to settle. Quiet your thoughts as you let them flow. Don't think about anything in particular as you relax very deeply. Feel your oneness with everything around you, how everything is part of the flow of your life. Be without thought, in this moment, free and at peace. The winds of chi are stirring within you. Let them sweep you toward a positive destiny.

Use what you have well and nothing will hold you back! Turn to your meditation regularly, even for a moment throughout your day. Gather yourself meditatively and let meditation guide you on your life's journey so that you are steady, balanced, and creatively expressing your unique nature as you stay on your path!

Conclusion: Moving Forward

Nurture balance using your meditative skills to keep yourself attuned. Have faith in your strong, capable nature, your Tao, which is filled with potential. You have unique talents that want to be expressed. And even though your nature may be obscured at times by the dark shadows of your moods, like the sun hidden behind the clouds, it's always there. If you follow the Tao, trusting your own deeper nature and that in the world, then even in shadowy moments of uncertainty and fear, the dark shadows will clear. May the hidden light of your awareness brighten your way, bringing happiness and fulfillment!

Recommended Reading

Simpkins, A. M., and C. A. Simpkins. 2011. *Meditation and Yoga in Psychotherapy: Techniques for Clinical Practice*. Hoboken, NJ: John Wiley and Sons.

Simpkins, C. A., and A. M. Simpkins. 1999. *Simple Taoism: A Guide to Living in Balance*. Rutland, VT: Tuttle Publishing.

———. 1999. *Simple Zen: A Guide to Living Moment by Moment*. Rutland, VT: Tuttle Publishing.

———. 2000. *Simple Buddhism: A Guide to Enlightened Living*. Rutland, VT: Tuttle Publishing.

———. 2007. *Meditation from Thought to Action with Audio CD*. San Diego, CA: Radiant Dolphin Press.

———. 2009. *Meditation for Therapists and Their Clients*. New York: W. W. Norton and Company.

———. 2010. *The Dao of Neuroscience: Eastern and Western Principles for Optimal Therapeutic Change*. New York: W. W. Norton and Company.

———. 2012. *Zen Meditation in Psychotherapy: Techniques for Clinical Practice*. Hoboken, NJ: John Wiley and Sons.

References

Abela, J. R., and D. U. D'Alessandro. 2002. "Beck's Cognitive Theory of Depression: A Test of the Diathesis-Stress and Causal Mediation Components." *British Journal of Clinical Psychology* 41:111–28.

American Psychiatric Association (APA). 2000. *Diagnostic and Statistical Manual of Mental Disorders: DSM-IV-TR*. 4th ed. Text rev. Arlington, VA: American Psychiatric Association.

Antonuccio, D. O., W. G. Danton, and G. Y. DeNelsky. 1995. "Psychotherapy versus Medication for Depression: Challenging the Conventional Wisdom with Data." *Professional Psychology: Research and Practice* 26 (6):574–85.

Ball, J. R., P. B. Mitchell, J. C. Corry, A. Skillecorn, M. Smith, and G. S. Malhi. 2006. "A Randomized Controlled Trial of Cognitive Therapy for Bipolar Disorder: Focus on Long-Term Change." *Journal of Clinical Psychiatry* 67 (2):277–86.

Barnhofer, T., C. Crane, E. Hargus, M. Amarasinghe, R. Winder, and J. M. Williams. 2009. "Mindfulness-Based Cognitive Therapy as a Treatment for Chronic Depression: A Preliminary Study." *Behaviour Research and Therapy* 47 (5):366–73.

Benes, F. M., S. L. Vincent, and M. Todtenkopf. 2001. "The Density of Pyramidal and Nonpyramidal Neurons in Anterior Cingulate Cortex of Schizophrenic and Bipolar Subjects." *Biological Psychiatry* 50 (6):395–406.

Benson, H. 1975. *The Relaxation Response*. New York: William Morrow and Company.

Benson, H., B. A. Rosner, B. R. Marzetta, and H. P. Klemchuk. 1974. "Decreased Blood Pressure in Borderline Hypertensive Subjects Who Practiced Meditation." *Journal of Chronic Diseases* 27 (3):163–69.

Bremner, J. D. 2005. *Brain Imaging Handbook*. New York: W. W. Norton and Company.

Briones, T. L., A. Y. Klintsova, and W. T. Greenough. 2004. "Stability of Synaptic Plasticity in the Adult Rat Visual Cortex Induced by Complex Environment Exposure." *Brain Research* 1018 (1):130–35.

Chuang Tzu. 1968. *The Complete Works of Chuang Tzu*. Translated by B. Watson. New York: Columbia University Press.

Colom, F., and D. Lam. 2005. "Psychoeducation: Improving Outcomes in Bipolar Disorder." *European Psychiatry* 20 (5–6):359–64.

Cooke, S. F., and T. V. Bliss. 2006. "Plasticity in the Human Central Nervous System." *Brain* 129 (pt. 7):1659–73.

Daban, C., E. Vieta, P. Mackin, and A. H. Young. 2005. "Hypothalamic-Pituitary-Adrenal Axis and Bipolar Disorder." *Psychiatric Clinics of North America* 28 (2):469–80.

Derntl, B., E. M. Seidel, I. Kryspin-Exner, A. Hasmann, and M. Dobmeier. 2009. "Facial Emotion Recognition in Patients with Bipolar I and Bipolar II Disorder." *British Journal of Clinical Psychology* 48 (pt. 4):363–75.

Dillbeck, M. C., P. D. Assimakis, D. Raimondi, D. W. Orme-Johnson, and R. Rowe. 1986. "Longitudinal Effects of the Transcendental Meditation and TM-Sidhi Program on Cognitive Ability and Cognitive Style." *Perceptual and Motor Skills* 62 (3):731–38.

Dillbeck, M. C., and D. W. Orme-Johnson. 1987. "Physiological Differences between Transcendental Meditation and Rest." *American Psychologist* 42 (9):879–881.

Duman, R. S. 2002. "Pathophysiology of Depression: The Concept of Synaptic Plasticity." *European Psychiatry* 17 (Suppl. 3):306–310.

Duman, R. S., and L. M. Monteggia. 2006. "A Neurotrophic Model for Stress-Related Mood Disorders." *Biological Psychiatry* 59 (12):1116–27.

Dumoulin, H. 1988. *Zen Buddhism: A History*. Vol. 1. Translated by J. W. Heisig and P. Knitter. New York: Macmillan.

El-Badri, S. M., D. A. Cousins, S. Parker, H. C. Ashton, V. L. McAllister, I. N. Ferrier, and P. B. Moore. 2006. "Magnetic Resonance Imaging Abnormalities in Young Euthymic Patients with Bipolar Affective Disorder." *British Journal of Psychiatry* 189:81–82.

Ellis, A., and D. J. Ellis. 2011. *Rational Emotive Behavior Therapy*. 3rd ed. Washington, DC: American Psychological Association.

Ellicott, A., C. Hammen, M. Gitlin, G. Brown, and K. Jamison. 1990. "Life Events and the Course of Bipolar Disorder." *American Journal of Psychiatry* 147 (9):1194–98.

Feldman, J. L., G. S. Mitchell, and E. E. Nattie. 2003. "Breathing: Rhythmicity, Plasticity, Chemosensitivity." *Annual Review of Neuroscience* 26:239–66. doi:10.1146/annurev.neuro.26.041002 .131103.

Freud, S. (1923) 1961. *The Ego and the Id*. Translated and edited by J. Strachey. New York: W. W. Norton and Company.

Goleman, D. J., and G. E. Schwartz. 1976. "Meditation as an Intervention in Stress Reactivity." *Journal of Consulting and Clinical Psychology* 44 (3):456–66.

Goodrich, D. E., and A. M. Kilbourne. 2010. "A Long Time Coming: The Creation of an Evidence Base for Physical Activity Prescription to Improve Health Outcomes in Bipolar Disorder." *Mental Health and Physical Activity* 3 (1):1–3.

Goodwin, F. K., and K. R. Jamison. 2007. *Manic-Depressive Illness: Bipolar Disorders and Recurrent Depression*. 2nd ed. New York: Oxford University Press.

Grant, J. A., J. Courtemanche, E. G. Duerden, G. H. Duncan, and P. Rainville. 2010. "Cortical Thickness and Pain Sensitivity in Zen Meditators." *Emotion* 10 (1):43–53.

Greenough, W. T., J. E. Black, and C. S. Wallace. 1987. "Experience and Brain Development." *Child Development* 58 (3):539–59.

Grossman P., L. Niemann, S. Schmidt, and H. Walach. 2004. "Mindfulness-Based Stress Reduction and Health Benefits: A Meta-analysis." *Journal of Psychosomatic Research* 57 (1):35–43.

Hebb, D. O. 1949. *The Organization of Behavior: A Neurophsychological Theory.* New York: John Wiley and Sons.

Holmes, E. A., J. R. Geddes, F. Colom, and G. M. Goodwin. 2008. "Mental Imagery as an Emotional Amplifier: Application to Bipolar Disorder." *Behaviour Research and Therapy* 46 (12):1251–58.

Holmes, E. A., and A. Mathews. 2010. "Mental Imagery in Emotion and Emotional Disorders." *Clinical Psychology Review* 30 (3):349–62.

Hölzel, B., J. Carmody, M. Vangel, C. Congleton, S. M. Yerramsetti, T. Gard, and S. W. Lazar. 2011. "Mindfulness Practice Leads to Increases in Regional Brain Gray Matter Density." *Psychiatry Research: Neuroimaging* 191:36–43.

Hugdahl, K. 1996. "Cognitive Influences on Human Autonomic Nervous System Function." *Current Opinion in Neurobiology* 6 (2):252–258.

Janis, I. L. 1971. *Stress and Frustration.* New York: Harcourt Brace Jovanovich.

Jerath, R., J. W. Edry, V. A. Barnes, and V. Jerath. 2006. "Physiology of Long Pranayamic Breathing: Neural Respiratory Elements May Provide a Mechanism That Explains How Slow, Deep Breathing Shifts the Autonomic Nervous System." *Medical Hypotheses* 67 (3):566–71.

Johnson, S. 1966. *Samuel Johnson: Rasselas, Poems, and Selected Prose.* Edited with an introduction and notes by B. H. Bronson. New York: Holt, Rinehart, and Winston.

Kabat-Zinn, J. 2003. "Mindfulness-Based Interventions in Context: Past, Present, and Future." *Clinical Psychology: Science and Practice* 10 (2):144–56.

Kennard, B. D., G. J. Emslie, T. L. Mayes, J. Nightingale-Teresi, P. A. Nakonezny, J. L. Hughes, J. M. Jones, R. Tao, S. M. Stewart, and R. B. Jarrett. 2008. "Cognitive-Behavioral Therapy to Prevent Relapse in Pediatric Responders to Pharmacotherapy for Major Depressive Disorder." *Journal of the American Academy of Child Adolescent Psychiatry* 47 (12):1395–1404.

Kohr, R. L. 1977. "Dimensionality in the Meditative Experience: A Replication." *Journal of Transpersonal Psychology* 9 (2):193–203.

Lagopoulos, J., J. Xu, I. Rasmussen, A. Vik, G. S. Malhi, C. F. Eliassen, I. E. Arntsen, J. G. Saether, S. Hollup, A. Holen, S. Davanger, and Ø. Ellingsen. 2009. "Increased Theta and Alpha EEG Activity during Nondirective Meditation." *Journal of Alternative and Complementary Medicine* 15 (11):1187–92.

Lao-tzu. 1985. *Tao Te Ching: The Book of Meaning and Life.* Translated by R. Wilhelm and H. G. Ostwald. London: Arkana.

———. 1989. *Te-Tao Ching: A New Translation Based on the Recently Discovered Ma-Wang Tui Texts.* Translated by R. G. Henricks. New York: Ballantine Books.

Lazar, S. W., G. Bush, R. L. Gollub, G. L. Fricchione, G. Khalsa, and H. Benson. 2000. "Functional Brain Mapping of the Relaxation Response and Meditation." *NeuroReport* 11 (7):1581–85.

Lazar, S. W., C. E. Kerr, R. H. Wasserman, J. R. Gray, D. N. Greve, M. T. Treadway, M. McGarvey, B. T. Quinn, J. A. Dusek, H. Benson, S. L. Rauch, C. I. Moore, and B. Fischl. 2005. "Meditation Experience Is Associated with Increased Cortical Thickness." *NeuroReport* 16 (17):1893–97.

Lembke, A., and T. A. Ketter. 2002. "Impaired Recognition of Facial Emotion in Mania." *American Journal of Psychiatry* 159:302–4.

Lutz, A., L. L. Greischar, N. B. Rawlings, M. Ricard, and R. J. Davidson. 2004. "Long-Term Meditators Self-Induce High-Amplitude Gamma Synchrony during Mental Practice." *Proceedings of the National Academy of Sciences* 101 (46):16369–73.

Lutz, A., H. A. Slagter, N. B. Rawlings, A. D. Francis, L. L. Greischar, and R. J. Davidson. 2009. "Mental Training Enhances Attentional Stability: Neural and Behavioral Evidence." *Journal of Neuroscience* 29 (42):13418–427.

Merikangas, K. R., H. S. Akiskal, J. Angst, P. E. Greenberg, R. M. A. Hirschfeld, M. Petukhova, and R. C. Kessler. 2007. "Lifetime and 12-Month Prevalence of Bipolar Spectrum Disorder in the National Comorbidity Survey Replication." *Archives of General Psychitary* 64 (5):543–52.

Meyer, A. 1948. *The Commonsense Psychiatry of Dr. Adolph Meyer: Fifty-Two Selected Papers.* Edited by Alfred Lief. New York: McGraw Hill.

Miller, J. J., K. Fletcher, and J. Kabat-Zinn. 1995. "Three-Year Follow-Up and Clinical Implications of a Mindfulness Meditation–Based Stress Reduction Intervention in the Treatment of Anxiety Disorders." *General Hospital Psychiatry* 17 (3):192–200.

Ming, Z., trans. 2001. *The Medical Classic of the Yellow Emperor.* Beijing, China: Foreign Languages Press.

Murray, G., and S. L. Johnson. 2010. "The Clinical Significance of Creativity in Bipolar Disorder." *Clinical Psychology Review* 30 (6):721–32.

National Institute of Mental Health (NIMH). 2012. *Bipolar Disorder.* www.nimh.nih.gov/health/publications/bipolar-disorder/complete-index.shtml (accessed June 19, 2012).

Paulus, M. P., C. Rogalsky, A. Simmons, J. S. Feinstein, and M. B. Stein. 2003. "Increased Activation in the Right Insula during Risk-Taking Decision Making Is Related to Harm Avoidance and Neuroticism." *NeuroImage* 19:1439–48.

Perls, F. S. 1969. *Gestalt Therapy Verbatim*. Lafayette, CA: Real People Press.

Post, R. M., and G. S. Leverich. 2008. *Treatment of Bipolar Illness: A Casebook for Physicians and Patients*. New York: W. W. Norton and Company.

Ramachandran, V. S. 2011. *The Tell-Tale Brain: A Neuroscientist's Quest for What Makes Us Human*. New York: W. W. Norton and Company.

Ramachandran, V. S., and S. Blakeslee. 1999. *Phantoms in the Brain: Probing the Mysteries of the Human Mind*. New York: Harper Perennial.

Schloesser, R. J., J. Huang, P. S. Klein, and H. K. Manji. 2008. "Cellular Plasticity Cascades in the Pathophysiology and Treatment of Bipolar Disorder." *Neuropsychopharmacology* 33 (1):110–33.

Seligman, M. E., and S. F. Maier. 1967. "Failure to Escape Traumatic Shock." *Journal of Experimental Psychology* 74 (1):1–9.

Selye, H. 1975. *Stress without Distress*. New York: Signet.

Strakowski, S. M., M. P. DelBello, K. W. Sax, M. E. Zimmerman, P. K. Shear, J. M. Hawkins, and E. R. Larson. 1999. "Brain Magnetic Resonance Imaging of Structural Abnormalities in Bipolar Disorder." *Archives of General Psychiatry* 56 (3):254–60.

Suzuki, S. 1970. *Zen Mind, Beginner's Mind*. Edited by T. Dixon. Introduction by R. Baker. New York: Walker/Weatherhill.

Tang, Y.-Y., Q. Lu, X. Geng, E. A. Stein, Y. Yang, and M. I. Posner. 2010. "Short-Term Meditation Induces White Matter Changes in the Anterior Cingulate." *Proceedings of the National Academy of Sciences* 107 (35):15649–52.

Tang, Y.-Y., Y. Ma, Y. Fan, H. Feng, J. Wang, S. Feng, Q. Lu, B. Hu, Y. Lin, J. Li, Y. Zhang, Y. Wang, L. Zhou, and M. Fan. 2009. "Central and Autonomic Nervous System Interaction Is Altered by Short-Term Meditation." *Proceedings of the National Academy of Sciences* 106 (22):8865–70.

Tang, Y.-Y., M. Yinghua, J. Wang, Y. Fan, S. Feng, Q. Lu, Q. Yu, D. Sui, M. K. Rothbart, M. Fan, and M. I. Posner. 2007. "Short-Term Meditation Training Improves Attention and Self-Regulation." *Proceedings of the National Academy of Sciences* 104 (43):17152–56.

Travis, F., and J. Shear. 2010. "Focused Attention, Open Monitoring, and Automatic Self-Transcending: Categories to Organize Meditations from Vedic, Buddhist, and Chinese Traditions." *Consciousness and Cognition* 19 (4):1110–18.

Waley, A., trans. and ed. 1958. *The Way and Its Power: Lao Tzu's Tao Tê Ching and Its Place in Chinese Thought.* New York: Grove Press.

Williams, J. M. G., and W. Kuyken. 2012. "Mindfulness-Based Cognitive Therapy: A Promising New Approach to Preventing Depressive Relapse." *British Journal of Psychiatry* 200:359–60. doi:10.1192/bjp.bp.111.104745.

C. Alexander Simpkins, PhD, and **Annellen M. Simpkins, PhD**, are psychologists specializing in meditation, hypnotherapy, and neuroscience. The Simpkins are authors of twenty-seven books, including a number of titles on Taoism: *Simple Taoism*, *Tao in Ten*, and most recently, *The Dao of Neuroscience*. They also have authored many books on the therapeutic application of meditation, including *Zen Meditation in Psychotherapy*, *Meditation and Yoga in Psychotherapy*, and *Meditation for Therapists and Their Clients*. In addition, they have a newly released book on neuroscience, *Neuroscience for Clinicians*. Their books have been published in more than twenty foreign editions and have won many awards.

The Simpkins regularly present seminars on meditation, hypnosis, and neuroscience worldwide to professionals and the public, and have performed research on therapeutic effectiveness using unconscious methods. Currently, the Simpkins are engaged in research on the unconscious movement. They practice and teach their own martial art, Tae Chun Do, combining meditation with movement. They reside in San Diego, California.

MORE BOOKS *from*
NEW HARBINGER PUBLICATIONS

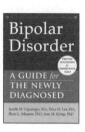

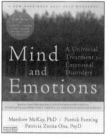

FROM OUR PUBLISHER—

As the publisher at New Harbinger and a clinical psychologist since 1978, I know that emotional problems are best helped with evidence-based therapies. These are the treatments derived from scientific research (randomized controlled trials) that show what works. Whether these treatments are delivered by trained clinicians or found in a self-help book, they are designed to provide you with proven strategies to overcome your problem.

Therapies that aren't evidence-based—whether offered by clinicians or in books—are much less likely to help. In fact, therapies that aren't guided by science may not help you at all. That's why this New Harbinger book is based on scientific evidence that the treatment can relieve emotional pain.

This is important: if this book isn't enough, and you need the help of a skilled therapist, use the following resources to find a clinician trained in the evidence-based protocols appropriate for your problem. And if you need more support—a community that understands what you're going through and can show you ways to cope—resources for that are provided below, as well.

Real help is available for the problems you have been struggling with. The skills you can learn from evidence-based therapies will change your life.

Matthew McKay, PhD
Publisher, New Harbinger Publications

new harbinger
CELEBRATING
40 YEARS

**If you need a therapist, the following organization
can help you find a therapist trained in cognitive behavioral therapy (CBT).**
The Association for Behavioral & Cognitive Therapies (ABCT) Find-a-Therapist service offers a list of therapists schooled in CBT techniques. Therapists listed are licensed professionals who have met the membership requirements of ABCT and who have chosen to appear in the directory.
Please visit www.abct.org and click on *Find a Therapist*.

**For additional support for patients, family, and friends,
please contact the following:**
Bipolar Happens
Visit www.bipolarhappens.com
Depression and Bipolar Support Alliance (DBSA)
Visit www.dbsalliance.org
National Alliance on Mental Illness (NAMI)
Please visit www.nami.org